GW00493072

CONSIDERING ADOPTION

SARAH BIGGS has previously written books about subfertility and at present she serves with the Inspectorate of The Human Fertilisation and Embryology Authority. She is married with two adopted sons and works as a Marketing and Training Consultant.

Overcoming Common Problems Series

For a full list of titles please contact
Sheldon Press, Marylebone Road, London NW1 4DU

Overcoming Common Problems Series

Overcoming Common Problems Series

Overcoming Common Problems

Considering Adoption?

Sarah Biggs

First published in Great Britain in 2000
Sheldon Press,
Holy Trinity Church
Marylebone Road
London NW1 4DU

British Library Cataloguing-in-Publication Data

A catalogue record for this book is available from the British Library

ISBN 0–85969–791–6

Typeset by Deltatype Limited, Birkenhead, Merseyside
Printed in Great Britain by
Biddles Ltd, Guildford and King's Lynn

Contents

Introduction

Whether you already have your own children and want to complete your family through adoption, or whether you are considering adoption as the only way you can have the children you dream of, this book sets out to explain the process in the United Kingdom today. Whether you ultimately adopt a baby of a few weeks old or an older child or sibling group, life will never be the same again.

This book is divided into two parts; the first deals with the processes you must undergo in order to adopt, the second outlines some of the issues that might confront you and your family after adoption.

There are many shortcomings within the system, but if you do adopt, your child will bring joy and fulfilment as well as the problems and responsibility that all parenthood implies.

I am indebted to the many people who helped me with material for this book, particularly the birth mothers, adopted children and adopters who shared their stories with me. I would particularly like to thank Ged Carmody, Janet Alvis, Sue Carpenter, Gill Fifield, Jennifer George, Jenny Goodman, Kath McCann and all the other contributors who preferred not to be named.

I would also like to remember the enormous contribution made towards the understanding of the suffering caused by infertility by Professor Mike Hull, of Bristol University, who died in 1999.

1

The changing face of adoption

In the 1970s several thousand babies were placed for adoption each year in England and Wales. Infertility management was primitive by today's standards, and once the available methods of medical intervention were exhausted it was natural that couples would look to adoption as a means of completing their families. Recently, however, fewer than 300 babies have been placed for adoption each year, while around 30,000 older children may be in the care of the local authorities. A small number of children are adopted by known relatives or step parents. As many as 10,000 older children or children with special needs are placed temporarily or permanently into the care system with a view to finding a permanent adoptive placement with a new family. There have never been so many children in care as there are today. There is also an increasing demand for homes for sibling groups of three, four or more children.

The major shifts in social attitudes since the sixties and seventies have removed the stigma attached to single, unmarried motherhood. The availability of efficient contraception and easier access to pregnancy termination have meant that far fewer babies are placed for adoption.

Many of the case histories reported in this book come from those children placed for adoption at a time when single parenting was not as commonplace as today. It may be easier for adopted children to reconcile themselves to the fact of their adoption when they realize that their birth mother had little or no option but to place them for adoption. With no such stigma today, will children find it harder to accept their adoption? How will you explain adoption to your child and what difficulties might you face in the future?

Adoption is no longer treated as a big secret, known to very few people, maybe only to the agency placing the child and to the adoptive couple, in many cases not even the adopted child being aware of the fact of their adoption until later life. Today's adoptive parents are expected to share the facts of adoption with their adopted child, recognize the child's past history and origins and help them come to terms with their adoption.

You may be looking at adoption to fulfil your dreams of a family but it is equally important to consider what you have to offer to a child. It is of paramount importance to understand that the needs of adopted and fostered children are, and must be, the primary consideration in the processes surrounding adoption. While we may look at adoption as a joyous occasion we must not lose sight of the fact that all of those involved have suffered a profound loss. The birth mother has lost her child and you may have suffered the loss of the child you never had, through infertility. But the greatest loss of all is suffered by the child who has lost his mother. The child is the one person in the adoption circle who has no choices.

This book is intended as an overview of the subject of adoption in the UK today, providing help, practical advice and support for those wishing to know more about it. The complex and often painful feelings associated with adoption are explored and experiences of others whose lives have been affected by adoption are given. You may ultimately conclude that adoption is not for you, but for many adoption is the answer, and while it may not always be an easy ride it brings enormous joy.

Who is responsible for adoption?

It is difficult to decide when one family is unfit or unable to care for a child and that that child would be better cared for elsewhere; or how best to advise parents who feel unable or unwilling to care for their child. This task falls to the local Social Services department.

It becomes even more difficult to establish who might be suitable parents for children in care, or which children may be freed for adoption with the consent of their birth parents. In the United Kingdom the agencies responsible for most aspects of adoption are regional Social Services, and a small number of voluntary agencies operating within largely the same remit.

The government department responsible for children in care, adoption and fostering is the Department of Health. The laws affecting adoption changed significantly with the introduction of the Child Protection Act and there have been recent moves to streamline and speed up adoption procedures for children in the United Kingdom, and to clarify guidelines for children adopted from overseas.

While adoption agencies are looking for couples in a stable relationship probably under the age of 30 to adopt the very few babies who become available for adoption each year, many agencies will be willing to consider single people, gay and lesbian individuals or couples as well as disabled and older individuals and couples as potential adopters who have much to offer children with particular needs. It is not necessary to be wealthy, own your own home or be in full time employment before you can be considered to adopt. You must consider, however, that if your home circumstances are under strain, bringing a child into that environment through adoption may not be appropriate.

Is adoption the answer for you?

Irrespective of the kind of child you are hoping to adopt, if you have been childless until now, take some time to look objectively at yourself to affirm that adoption is going to be the right option for you and any child who might come into your life. If your lifestyle has become established in a way that children and the traumas they will bring may disrupt and disturb it too much, then maybe adoption is not the right course for you. Caring for a pet successfully may be a good grounding for understanding the commitment required to care for a child.

Whatever your motive for considering adoption, you should ask yourself the following questions at the outset. Through the adoption process others will be asking you the same questions, and will be looking for positive answers.

- Do you like children?
- Do you expect children to conform to your own standards, or are you flexible enough to allow them to be themselves, perhaps with a set of values which do not accord with your own?
- Is your partner wholly supportive of this initiative, or is it you who are leading the way? If so make sure that your partner is supportive, otherwise social workers may be put off.

- If you are single do you have the support of family and friends who will help you when you need it?
- Do you accept that a child may not be grateful to you and may not learn to love you for a very long time?
- Are there aspects of behaviour in a child which you would find unacceptable, such as dishonesty or sexual precocity?
- Could you cope with a child who may have specific learning difficulties, mental or physical handicap? Could you cope with a child who failed to reach your expectations intellectually or physically?
- Can you give the space to a child to understand and know their past and to have affection for those who have been close to them before, such as birth or foster parents or siblings placed elsewhere?
- Can you accept that a child may disrupt your life, your activities, your relationship with your partner and your home?
- Do you accept that children who come into your life through adoption are not the same as children you may have naturally?
- Can other children in your family cope with a newcomer?
- Are you prepared to end fertility treatment if your application is accepted?
- Are you prepared for the intrusion that assessment by a social worker will bring?

If you feel that you can answer all those questions positively, or that you are aware of your own limitations and feel that you will be able to deal with the very real problems and stresses that will happen, then read on. If, realistically, you feel that your expectations may just be too high, or that maybe you have been childless too long to cope with the major upheaval and change that bringing a child into your life will mean, whether it is a baby or an older child, then maybe adoption is not the answer for you.

Do not enter into the adoption arena believing that an adopted child will have the same relationship with you that a child born to you would have – accept that it will be different, not better and not worse, but as fulfilling and in many ways more fulfilling. When a child is born to you it is like a sheet of paper with the lines drawn, genetic lines which will dictate where the writing and the pictures appear. Your child would have some of your traits and your partner's, including some of your own faults and shortcomings. The adopted child is a blank sheet which will fill up with unimaginable lines and colours in a wealth of mutual discovery.

No one is expecting you to be a perfect parent. There is no such thing as a perfect parent; many will say you just have to be good enough. Without doubt, adopting a child means that you will have to try harder, give more and expect less than a natural parent. With support, a sense of humour and good preparation, however, you can transform the life of a child and offer them a secure and loving home. Expect that sometimes you may do the wrong thing and have the strength to seek help when you need it. If there are problems it is not a sign of failure and not your fault. For all the times you get it wrong there will be a hundred times you get it right.

For those with no children

The majority of people contacting Social Services about baby adoption fear they may be infertile. It has been suggested that approximately 40,000 couples present to their general practitioner each year concerned about their fertility. Many of these couples may already have one or more children. While the pain of subfertility for them is just as great as for those who have no children, adoption may not seem to be such a high priority. If you have always dreamed of the child you will have, whether it is a second child, a child of your new partner or your first child, the slow realization that this may not become a reality is a painful process.

There is a fundamental difference between infertility and childlessness and it is important to recognize that difference before moving on towards adoption. Infertility has almost nothing to do with whether or not a man or woman has a child. It is a deeply personal grief arising from the inability to father or bear a child. A primitive, natural and indefinable urge causes most of us to want to reproduce, and if we find we cannot, our image of ourselves is altered. We are forced to examine our role in the world, adjust our life plan. Will we fulfil the dreams and expectations that have formed a crucial part of our make-up since childhood? Modern assisted conception techniques take control away while offering hope, which may continue for years without success. Our self-esteem falters and our relationships with friends and family members may suffer. Many couples keep their infertility secret from all but the most intimate of friends and feel stigmatized by their failure to gain entrance to the cosy family club.

In time it is possible to come to terms with infertility and move on. Counselling will help enormously in focussing on the anger, grief, depression and despair which are the natural consequences of infertility. Acceptance and understanding of these feelings is the key to coming to terms with them. This must happen before you can begin to contemplate adoption. The adopted child must never be second best.

It is possible to come to terms with infertility and accept that children will not form a part of your life, and to find other fulfilment, whether through career, a change in lifestyle or through pets. Childlessness, however, is a different issue. Many individuals and couples are childless by design, feeling no great sense of deprivation or loss, but for some the physical fact of childlessness is a great burden. Such people feel that there is something missing in their life, something physical that should be there.

Childlessness is the physical effect of not having a child in your life; *infertility* is an emotional issue which may affect you even if you already have a child. You can come to terms with infertility but if you are not going to have a child of your own the only way to overcome childlessness is through adoption. Adoption is a solution for childlessness; it is not the cure for infertility.

Counselling support

It is vital that you identify and explore your feelings about being unable to have your own child. These will inevitably surface at some point in your life, such as when a friend announces a pregnancy, or when family members ask about your plans for a family or just when another period arrives. These deep, searing feelings should not surface after adoption because they will interfere with the bonding process with a new child who is not the child you are grieving for. Counselling support, despite the apparent stigma some may feel is attached to it, can help enormously in dealing with the powerful and destructive feelings wrought by infertility and childlessness. These feelings are not only normal and understandable but it would be strange if they were not manifest in both men and women at different times and in different ways.

Without doubt, the passage of time will help reconcile most people to their infertility and they will be able to move on to a fulfilling future, but as time is an issue in adoption, this process can be accelerated through counselling, maybe even just one or two sessions. If you are going to consider taking into your life a child who is not born to you, you must be prepared to accept their needs and crises. You will be best able to do this if you have come to terms with your own loss.

Any number of people may be able to help you explore your feelings about your infertility – a friend, a close relative, or a religious adviser. There are many support groups and professional counsellors whose main expertise is in the area of infertility. It may be possible for social workers to talk to you and your partner to explore your feelings about infertility and adoption, but financial pressures mean that Social Services are severely stretched and it may not be possible for them to see you in person.

It is important to grieve for the child you may never have before you can begin to move towards acceptance and ultimately the desire to adopt a child who will be the child you want, not the child you might have had. Having accepted that you may not have your own child, you must move towards an awareness of just what is involved in adoption. Only you can decide whether or not adoption will fulfil your needs and, more importantly, whether you can meet the needs of the adopted child.

This process is long and painful and all couples must have passed through it before social workers can begin to consider them as adoptive parents. In the days when there were many children available for adoption and screening processes were less exhaustive, children who were adopted did not always have a happy life, perhaps for a variety of reasons.

Shirley

'I was adopted after the death of my mother's two-year-old daughter. She had two sons and wanted to replace her lost daughter. All through my life she told me how lucky I was to have all the things she had given me and how grateful I should be. I knew she felt I had never come close to the daughter she had lost and was disappointed in me.'

It is not good for your adopted child if your desire to have your own child has not been dealt with. There have been cases where couples have adopted a child and yet continued, through treatment, to try for a child of their own. While this does not mean the adopted child is not loved, it may be an indication that adoption was not the solution to the needs of the couple and may leave the adopted child feeling different and less well loved than a child who results from subsequent treatment.

It also happens, not uncommonly, that couples diagnosed as having unexplained infertility may adopt and then fall pregnant naturally, but this is not the same as deliberately seeking treatment to have a natural child. It is for this reason that Social Services may want assurances from couples that medical investigation has indicated little or no likelihood of achieving pregnancy or that treatment has ended. Primarily, this is so that the small number of babies placed for adoption can be directed towards those least likely to have their own child.

Many adoption agency workers feel that they would ultimately like to place two children with each adoptive family so that an adopted child is not the only child in the family. Adopted siblings, that is brothers or sisters, even if they have no biological relationship to each other, will be able to share the experiences of their adoption with each other as they grow older.

Like many market-places, the adoption system operates on a supply and demand dynamic, and unfortunately there is a much greater demand than supply. For this reason Social Services are able to pick and choose those couples they will consider for baby adoption. Couples whom social workers deem not to have tried to come to terms with their infertility are unlikely to be accepted as potential adopters, so it is important to demonstrate that counselling support has been sought.

However, without the men and women coming forward to adopt the many children in their care, Social Services would find their work impossible, so don't undervalue your importance to them when you are considering how much you need their help to achieve your family.

When to make the first steps towards adoption

Many couples consider adoption when they are in the first throes of distress at their own failure to conceive. They may subsequently dismiss the idea in favour of exploring all treatment options first, and this is only wise. Many infertile men and women report that they have to feel they have done all they can to have a child before other options are contemplated. These options may include remaining childless. To arrive at the conclusion that you are not going to have your own child and that you strongly desire to adopt another person's child and love it as your own is a long and heartrending process taking many years.

One of the most agonizing features of infertility management is the constant awareness of the passing of time. Knowing that you are unlikely to be considered for adoption once you are past 30 is an additional pressure, prompting many couples to contact adoption agencies before they have completed fertility treatment.

This is a catch-22: if you leave it until you know you are ready then it may be too late to adopt a baby in this country. If you have not started trying for a family until later in life you may already be over the maximum age stipulated by adoption agencies for baby adopters. If you are still undergoing fertility treatment it is reasonable to explore the adoption procedure. If there is a waiting list, put your name on it; if there are exploratory meetings, attend them; but do not consider assessment until you have finished fertility treatment and are well on the way towards coming to terms with your infertility.

Claire

'After years of IVF treatment I was coming up to the ninth attempt at the age of 32. I felt that I was going to explode with the stresses of treatment. I was travelling to London, a round trip of over 100 miles for each visit, and I really felt that it wasn't going to happen for me, yet I was afraid to stop treatment, because I was on an NHS programme and it wasn't costing us the fortune many other couples were paying.

'Counselling had been suggested to me several times but I felt angry at the suggestion that I needed what I saw as psychological help, but I felt that I just couldn't cope any more.

'I found the number of a hypnotherapist and I decided that I would try hypnotherapy to help me change my attitude towards treatment and to help me calm down.

'When I saw the man we talked for a long time and I don't really understand whether or not I was hypnotized but suddenly it felt like the floodgates had opened and out poured all the grief I had been holding in for years about my infertility. I cried and cried. After about an hour, I guess, I left the room feeling as though a great weight had gone from my shoulders, as if there had been a big red room in my head full of rubbish which had now been cleared.

'I went just once more and it felt as though my emotions were less intense, although I cried again, and when I left I knew that I wouldn't need to go again. I went ahead with the last IVF, which didn't work, but this time I felt as though I could cope and I did. I had hoped the consultant would tell me that there was no use continuing with IVF and I was quite disappointed that he was prepared to keep going. I think for his research project he was interested to see how many times someone could have treatment before succeeding. This meant that I had to make the decision myself, yet strangely I found it quite an easy decision in the end. I felt so incredibly relieved to get off the treadmill after eight years of trying for a baby.

'I had already made several approaches about adoption but this time I knew that this was what I wanted and I was determined to succeed, which I did!'

Those who seek to adopt a child, irrespective of the age and circumstances of that child, must feel that this is the child they want over and above any other, not second best and not in place of another.

Couples who have not conceived within two years are generally referred for medical investigation and, if appropriate, subsequent treatment. Many of these couples will conceive over the next two years. With the advanced treatments available the majority of couples may achieve a pregnancy in time. This leaves a core of couples whose infertility cannot be overcome through treatment or who choose not to proceed with assisted conception treatment. If this group represents just 5 per cent of all couples who initially seek help from their doctor, based on the figure of 40,000 couples this may mean as many as 2000 couples considering adoption in any year.

Many couples may be deterred from considering adoption because they believe that baby adoption in the United Kingdom is a difficult and lengthy process. For this reason, particularly if they feel they may be over the maximum age permitted, they may persist with medical treatment or turn to overseas adoption as a first option.

Social workers report that they receive two or three calls each month from couples requesting information about baby adoption, and serious applications from as many as five times the number of potential adopters as there are babies available to adopt. Simple arithmetic demonstrates that, if fewer than 300 babies are placed each year, the majority of couples are destined to be disappointed. Even those who may ultimately succeed will be faced with a considerable wait.

Some couples know, at a fairly early stage in their relationship, that they will be unable to have a child of their own, perhaps through disability or hereditary, medical, or genetic factors, and that adoption is the only way they can have a family. For these couples adoption will appear on the agenda at a much earlier stage.

Allowing for the time taken to complete the necessary procedures prior to being considered as adoptive parents, and the subsequent wait for a child to become available, it becomes important to register an interest in adoption at an early stage, even if you subsequently decide not to proceed with your application.

At this point adoption agencies will try to separate the serious enquirer from those who are ambivalent or unsure. Since resources are limited and the assessment of prospective adopters is expensive, it would be pointless to assess people who will not follow the process through, or who stand little chance of adopting a child at the end of the process. The response to your enquiry may be a standard letter informing you that no babies are available for adoption currently but if you would like to discuss other opportunities you can attend a group meeting on a given date. You will find your attention directed towards the large number of older children or those with special needs who require adoption.

If you are serious about adoption, attend meetings and persist in your application. Those whose will to adopt is strong will endeavour to overcome initial barriers. You may need to keep contacting agencies by letter or telephone, but this will show them you are committed to the idea of adoption.

2

Social Services and the home assessment

Social Services

The Social Service system operates within the terms of the Welfare of the Child Act and the Adoption Act 1976 as well as Adoption Agencies Regulations 1983. There are set standards for the provision of adoption services to potential adopters, birth parents, adopted children and those who have already adopted. These include a requirement for local authorities to establish and maintain an adoption service designed to meet the needs of children, their birth parents or guardians and those who may adopt a child. They must

- have effective arrangements to advise, assess, counsel, and support those who become prospective adopters and those who do not;
- produce clear placement plans for all children placed for adoption reflecting their cultural and racial heritage;
- maintain records of their involvement with all parties, which should be confidential;
- ensure that all parties are familiar with the complaints procedure.

The 1976 Adoption Act imposes a statutory duty on adoption agencies to provide post-adoption support. There are also guidelines to ensure that a service is provided to those children who are placed from other countries.

This service is seen by many as an underfunded, under-resourced and imperfect system. Many prospective adopters feel that Social Services or the voluntary agency represent a barrier between them and their goal. While researching this book I received few positive endorsements of Social Services from any contributor and many damning indictments of both policy and practice from adopters, birth parents and foster carers. However, there are many happy stories where assessment and placement went well, where support was provided when it was needed both before and after adoption, and where the outcomes for the families were good. Maybe it is only to be expected that, with a growing list of children needing placement away from their birth families and an underfunded, under-resourced Social Services system, there will be fundamental shortcomings.

It falls to the social worker to decide when a child is at risk at home, and whether that child's needs would be better served by being removed from that home or allowed to remain. Social workers counsel pregnant women and mothers about the advisability of placing a child for adoption or fostering and they try to find the most appropriate family in which to place that child.

Policies on social issues do not stand still. In a changing society experience and research shed new light on age-old problems, leading to a shift in one direction or another. The current thinking on adoption policy has become polarized to reflect two extreme views. On the one hand, many social workers and policy makers believe that the needs of the child are best served by helping a mother to keep her child, providing support with financial resources and child care. On the other hand some believe that children who are unwanted, or for whom care systems may be inadequate, are better placed for adoption as soon as possible.

In effect this may occasionally mean that mothers who really cannot cope are left with babies too long. It may also mean that children are placed in temporary foster care either voluntarily or forcibly when birth parents are unable to cope or are found to be inadequate or neglectful. While this may ultimately result in successful reunion, the disruption to the child's attachment and development can be seriously affected. If a decision is made to place a child for adoption, valuable time has been lost, carers have been shifted and the child is faced with another disruptive and distressing move. It is no wonder that such children are deeply affected and often irreversibly damaged by their experiences.

Social Services are aware of the shortcomings of this system, and policies are moving towards running two programmes in parallel for such children, one designed to support the birth family in preparation for reunion and, simultaneously, a search for suitable adopters in case the support should fail. This may reduce the amount of time a child or sibling group spends in foster care and may, possibly, eliminate unnecessary moves. In the past these systems have run consecutively meaning that the time spent in care is extended from months to years.

It is important to understand the position of social workers in these situations. If they are seen to be actively taking children from their parents into a permanent adoptive placement, the birth parents may feel they have not been given time to adjust and cope. It must also be understood that, no matter what they have experienced at the hands of their parents, most young children love their parents unquestioningly and unconditionally, even if that care has included neglect and abuse, for that is the only care they know.

The system fails many children who are neither available for adoption nor remain with their families. Often these children are passed through a succession of foster homes until they become impossible to place permanently due to behavioural difficulties.

There should be no doubt that the removal of a child from its natural parent causes enormous pain to all parties, whether with their consent or otherwise, and irrespective of the age of the child. Even if all parties recognize that the life of the child has been enhanced by the placement, they must both become reconciled to their separation and loss. This is true even of those children who have been placed for adoption at a very early age.

Foster carers are a vital part of the network which provides support for children who cannot be cared for by their natural families. They receive a modest allowance for providing temporary care for children on behalf of the local authority. Often children are only in a foster home for a short time while parents are in crisis, sick or homeless. Sometimes this care extends for a much longer period which may culminate in a decision by the local authority and the natural parents to place the child in more permanent care. This may mean remaining with the foster family, if possible, or moving to another foster or care home while the adoption process is embarked upon.

Applying to adopt: what happens next?

If, as an individual or as a couple, you believe you have something to offer a child who needs a home, contact your local Social Services or a local adoption agency for the name of their family placement or adoption co-ordinator. For a complete list of adoption agencies, acquire a copy of *Adopting a Child: A Guide for People Interested in Adoption*, by Prue Chennells and Chris Hammond (available from British Agencies for Adoption and Fostering (address on p.117)). This gives an overview of adoption and fostering with a complete list of around 200 agencies which provide adoption services in England, Scotland, and Wales. These will usually be agencies run by your local authority but some are voluntary bodies and others may have a particular religious affiliation such as the Catholic Children's Society (although they do not usually restrict themselves to Catholic applicants). In Northern Ireland, contact your local Social Services Department.

This is a good time to join Adoption UK, the National Adoptive Parents Network, which supports families before, during and after adoption. The membership pack includes much valuable information including the following booklets: *Practical Steps to Adoption,* a *Checklist for Prospective Adopters,* and *Thinking about Adoption.* Adoption UK will also be able to put you in touch with others in your area with experience of adoption.

Local authority agencies may only be able to accept couples for assessment from within their regional boundaries, but some of the voluntary bodies may be able to accept couples from further afield. It is inadvisable to approach an agency which is far from home, because they will not only be helping you with the adoption process but, if you are successful, they will also be providing you with support after adoption. Find the nearest local authority agency and any other voluntary agency which is fairly near your home and any other which may have a religious affiliation the same as yours.

What kind of people can be considered for adoption?

For the few healthy babies available for adoption, agencies are looking for couples who can demonstrate a stable, happy relationship, who are married, have no previous children, are in good health, and where both partners are under the age of around 30–35 and over 21 years.

It is extremely unlikely that you will even be considered for baby adoption if you and your partner are not married, even if you are in a stable relationship. This does not mean that you would not be considered for adoption of an older child or a child with special needs, but you should understand that only one of you can be recognized as the legal parent.

As there are many children of black and mixed-race origins looking for a permanent home, couples of similar background are eagerly sought and whether or not you are married may not be such an issue, although it is still important that your relationship is stable.

You can still be considered for adoption if you do not have a partner, or if you already have natural children, or if you have a disability. Today Social Services are much more open to considering homosexual and lesbian individuals and couples as adopters too.

Birth certificates and marriage certificates (in addition to divorce certificates if applicable) have to be made available to social workers and the courts. To apply for the adoption order your domicile, that is the place you consider to be home even if for the time being you live or work elsewhere, must be within the United Kingdom. This might prove difficult for families where one or more members are in the forces or work overseas, so it is important to discuss this early on in your application. However, it should not necessarily exclude you from consideration for adoption.

At some point during the assessment process, your social worker will ask you to sign forms giving your permission for them to conduct a police enquiry to check for any previous convictions or cautions you may have received. It is not unknown for criminal convictions to come up in a name similar to yours, particularly if you have a common name, so you may be asked for more information regarding previous addresses and date of birth so they can eliminate that possibility.

If you have any previous convictions, the agency will use its own discretion about whether or not to proceed with an adoption assessment but any offences committed against children are very likely to exclude you forthwith. If there are other adult members of your household who would be living with you if you adopted a child, they too must consent to police checks.

What kind of children are there?

Children who become available for adoption come from a wide variety of ethnic, racial, religious and cultural backgrounds. Their parents may be middle class or working class. They can be any age from birth to teenage, single children or part of a larger sibling group. Few are orphans who have no living relatives, although a very small number of babies each year are foundlings, babies found abandoned for whom all hope of finding the birth mother has been lost. The only common factor is that the birth parents cannot, will not or should not have care of the child in the future.

You may see children advertised in local papers and television programmes; these children and their parents will have given their consent to be advertised.

What if I work?

The fact that you work should not stand in the way of your adopting a child, but you are unlikely to be considered for baby adoption if it is your intention to continue full time work or even part time work immediately after placement. Few employers will grant paid maternity leave to women who adopt a child of any age although it could be argued to be even more important for adopters to have time to bond with their new child. Many women have found it hard to keep their job after placement because of the short notice that is likely to be given before they must leave. Unlike the amount of time a pregnant woman has to prepare her workload for her absence, the suddenness of placement with adoption, even after years of waiting, is often only a few days or weeks notice and this requires a very sympathetic employer indeed, and one of you, if you have a partner, will need time to bond with the child you adopt.

This is not to say that you will never be able to return to work in time or that you may not be able to work part time, but social workers will expect you to set aside some time for parenting. You will require the flexibility to demonstrate that you will make that time available, even if it is at very short notice. Many couples find that, between them, they can set aside enough time for either one of them to be available to be with the child or children after placement.

19

What do I do next?

In the first instance telephone or write to the agencies you have identified. They will need to know about you and your partner, how long you have been married, your ages and history of infertility. It is unlikely that they will want any further information at this stage.

The agencies operate in many different ways. While some may invite you to a regular information meeting or preparation class, where you can learn more about the children available for adoption, others may operate a waiting list for potential adopters which may be open or closed. This is, effectively, a list for couples waiting to be considered for assessment, and because so few babies are available for adoption such lists may be closed for a period of years. If this is the case and they are prepared to put you on the list you must keep in contact with them over the ensuing years. Other agencies might invite couples to an informal meeting which might lead to a home assessment.

Although there may be a small number of black or mixed-race babies available for adoption, researchers have demonstrated that such children will be happier if placed with parents of similar origin and so efforts are made to match the children to the parents as much as possible, so if you or your partner are black or come from another ethnic or cultural background your chances of being considered for adoption of an infant from a similar background will be higher.

If you and your partner are in your late thirties or early forties agencies may ask you to consider the possibility of adopting an older child, a sibling group or a child with special needs.

Once you are clear about what is available and you feel ready to proceed you must notify the agency you have chosen, which will decide whether to take your application further. If they agree they will commission a home study. A social worker will be appointed who will visit you in your home or meet you in the Social Work department to study many aspects of your lives, your suitability for adoption and what kind of life you can offer a child. This is a lengthy and costly process which many find intrusive and stressful. Having reached this stage with one agency it is not helpful to try another in the hope of doubling your chances of adoption as, in practice, this will not prove to be the case.

The home study

During the course of the home study your social worker will be trying to understand you and discover what you have to offer a child, while at the same time helping you prepare for parenthood. You will need to consider and share with your assessor some fundamental questions about yourself. Who are the important people in your life and how do you relate to them? What are your interests, work and family background? What do you hope for in a family and from your adopted child? What is your lifestyle and how will it change through adoption?

What a difficult task it is to establish who is a suitable parent and who isn't! For the fertile no such assessments are made and it is very rare for parents to be considered so inadequate as to be unfit to care for their own children. Applicants feel, quite reasonably, that they are under scrutiny and that they must find the right answers for the questions they are asked. Nonetheless, society demands that rigorous measures are used to establish that children available for adoption are placed with suitable people.

The home study is designed to help the social worker know and understand you as a person, as part of a couple and as a potential parent. How do you perceive parenthood, how would your life change with a child? What do members of your extended family or other people who are important to you feel about the proposed adoption? What changes would be involved and how would you cope if your circumstances changed?

It is important for you to be open and honest about your expectations and feelings, your strengths and weaknesses. Many applicants find the assessment process enjoyable, helping them towards a realistic expectation of what adoption may bring. It is important that you trust your assessor and that they trust you.

It is a good exercise to sit down, both with your partner and on your own, to write down what you envisage your lives would be like with a family. Would one of you give up work? Who would undertake the bulk of the parenting? What experience have you had with other children, nephews, nieces, children of friends? What life experiences would you want to share with your family? What is important to you? What are your attitudes to education, religion, sport, and relationships? How will these fit in with your child? Write down what you think may happen in a normal week, what you remember about your own schooling, about your childhood, what was good and what was bad and what you would want your child's life to be like.

Rose and Ian

'We were very worried about the home study. We didn't really see eye to eye with the social worker assigned to us and felt she didn't think we were going to be suitable. We felt that we were too "middle class" for her. Eventually she moved on and we were assigned another social worker who was wonderful and we even began to enjoy the process, but all in all it took a long time and we were thrilled when we were finally approved.'

The social worker and you

It is helpful if you can develop a good relationship with your assessor, but if this does not happen, it does not mean that the social worker will be biased against you. Children for adoption come from a variety of backgrounds and so it is important that prospective adopters represent a variety of backgrounds so that an effective match can be made.

Mandy

'We felt that it would go against us because we lived in a council flat and didn't have good jobs. I sometimes felt that when I was answering her questions I should say what I thought she wanted to hear not what I really felt.'

The home study may take several months. During this time the social worker will ask you about your background, education, employment, interests, previous and present relationships. You will be asked about your experiences of childhood as well as what kind of childhood you would like to offer a child and how you would adapt your lifestyle to accommodate that child. Perhaps the most difficult question to answer is why you want to adopt a child.

You will need to consider what values you will bring to

22

parenting and how you might cope with the specific needs of a child. How will you discipline a child and respond to their particular needs?

You will need to consider the financial implications of adoption, particularly if you are going to give up work to become the primary caregiver or if you are going to need financial support from the adoption agency.

During the course of the home study the commissioning agency will require health and legal checks. Applicants are required to undergo a basic medical examination, usually by their own family doctor; this must be updated every two years until the child is placed with you. You will have to pay for this report, and are asked to give your consent for it to be sent to the assessing agency.

If you have a medical problem or disability this will not automatically exclude you from being considered as adopters, but if you smoke or drink to excess you can expect this to have an impact on your application. The principle behind the medical check is to take measures to ensure, as much as possible, that you will be likely to live a healthy life, long enough to see your adopted child into adulthood. There are obviously no guarantees that any of us will live into our eighties but there are some criteria which have been shown to cause ill health and premature death and these include obesity, drinking alcohol in excess and smoking.

Openness

Many issues have to be covered during the course of the home study and one of particular importance is the question of openness. It is now widely recognized that children who are adopted cope much better if they are aware of the fact of their adoption from an early age. There really is no good reason to keep it a secret and many reasons to be proud of being either an adoptive parent or an adopted child. In many ways, keeping adoption secret will involve a complicated web of deceit which may undermine the relationship between parent and child and ultimately cause immense distress to you both.

It is also increasingly common for some form of contact to be retained between the birth parents or extended family members and the adopted child, where this is not considered to be damaging for the child. This might take the form of occasional visits by a birth parent or birth grandparent, or a meeting of siblings, but in practice is much more likely to involve an exchange of letters (through a third party so that addresses are not disclosed) about the well-being of both the child and the birth parents. Your feelings about this eventuality will be explored.

Having said this, many birth mothers are so distressed following the placement of their child for adoption, even when it has been a voluntary decision so to do, that they choose to block the existence of their child from their mind. The law states that no attempt to trace a child or parent can commence before the child's eighteenth birthday, so for many children openness extends no further than telling them they are adopted and answering their questions, as well as you can, from the information you have.

If you are going to be open about adoption you are faced with the issue of explaining adoption to your child. Even if your child knows he is adopted, who else would you want to know? Will you want to keep it a secret from everyone outside the immediate family? How will you feel if you meet your child's birth parents? How will your friends and family cope with your adopted child? The social worker can help you through these areas.

Referees

At some point during the home study you will be asked to provide the names of two referees, who know you well and have known you for some time. The purpose of this is for the assessor to get another perspective on your relationship, your strengths and weaknesses and how your relationship might be affected by adopting a child.

Because your referees will need to speak honestly and openly about you, your social worker will talk to them privately and may not inform you of the outcome of that meeting. In one case a couple's referee confided that one of the partners had previously had an extramarital affair. This was not something the social worker was able to share with the couple, but she felt it was sufficient reason not to put forward the couple as adopters. It is important that referees share your enthusiasm for your adoption plans; if they express to the social worker reservations they have not shared with you, this may cause problems. Ask potential referees yourself whether they feel you would make good parents. If they have reservations about you or your partner, you need to know.

What if I am unhappy about the assessment?

Occasionally a couple feel that their particular assessor is not sympathetic to them and their viewpoint. It is difficult to try to get another social worker assigned as there are relatively few of them and Social Services are under strict financial pressures. Nonetheless, social workers have a clear complaints policy which they should outline to you and, in the event that you feel there have been shortcomings in the assessment process, you should take the measures suggested in their complaints procedure.

It is possible that the study leads the assessor to feel that you might not be ready for adoption, perhaps because she feels that you have not come to terms with your infertility or that your relationship may not withstand the pressures of a family. Your referees, who will have spoken in confidence to the assessor, may even have said they felt that you would be wholly unsuitable parents! If, during the home study period, the assessor feels strongly that adoption is not for you, this should become apparent before your application is submitted to the panel in your area which decides on the suitability of applicants as adopters. Your social worker should not put your case to panel if she feels it is unlikely to be successful. In that case, if you are determined, you can try another agency although they will need to be told of the reasons your application did not proceed with the first agency.

The agency assessing you has clear duties towards you which include keeping to the proposed time scale for completing an assessment, keeping appointments they have made with you, unless unavoidable, and keeping you informed throughout the process. If they feel that your application may be unsuccessful you should be told the reasons for this.

The home study report

The assessor will produce a detailed report based on his or her findings, which you will have an opportunity to read before it is submitted to an adoption panel. This report is based on form F, a six-page document completed by the social worker and the applicants. Much of the information is of a deeply personal and confidential nature.

The first page covers details of the assessing agency, your details and those of any other children in the family. The second page outlines the type of adoption or fostering sought along with a list of the type of child for whom applicants would like to be considered, specifying age range, number of children, gender, religion, and whether the children may have suffered sexual abuse, medical problems, severe learning difficulties, physical or mental disability, and those for whom development is uncertain. You will also be able to state whether you would be prepared to consider any form of contact with the birth family.

Through the assessment process you will explore aspects of all the children who might become available for adoption and whether or not your own experience, background or training equips you to care for a child with a particular history or disability. Next to each category are three letters: Y for Yes, N for No, L for Limited. With your social worker you will decide which categories you would definitely consider, which you would definitely not and which you would consider if the degree of disability, difficulty or damage caused by abuse were limited.

The next two pages are devoted to a profile of your family, which might be written in your own words, describing your lifestyle, personality, interests and experience. A photograph of your family is also included in this section. You may like to make a video, tape or book about your family which can be included with your application.

A description of your home and any proposed accommodation for a child follows, along with a description of your neighbourhood including ethnic mix, schools, transport, recreation and medical facilities in the vicinity.

Applicants should outline their availability to travel for introductions taking into account means of transport and work or social commitments as well as post-adoption support requirements.

The legal requirements include marital history, nationality and whether or not consideration can be given to adopting a child where there is a complicated legal history which might cause some delay in adoption.

The history of the assessment process for each family is described, including any special training undergone to prepare for a child with particular needs. If you have chosen to seek to adopt a child with a disability and you are relying on your family to provide vital support, bear in mind that one day older relatives, such as your parents, may need your support too and you may find yourself trying to cope with your child and elderly or sick parents at the same time.

Health issues are covered comprehensively, for each family member including any potentially inherited condition in extended family members. This should not automatically exclude you if a parent has an inheritable condition. If you have experience of a close family member with disability, or mental or emotional difficulty you may be better qualified to cope with similar disabilities in a child. Your attitudes to a child with physical or mental handicap or ill health are recorded.

Tim

'My mother is severely schizophrenic and so we felt that we would be happy to adopt a child where mental illness might have been an issue with the parents. We knew that if we had been able to have a child of our own, we would run at least a 25 per cent chance that our child might inherit the condition. Also we understand the condition better than people who have not been exposed to it before.'

If you have serious reservations about any potential problems a child may have, you must declare them at this stage. It is unlikely to affect your application adversely if you feel unhappy about a physical disability, for example, and much more important to state it at the outset rather than later. There are still many children available for adoption who are likely to be a good match for you.

Finally, form F includes the referees' reports and the social worker's assessment of the applicants. Once it has been completed you will see a copy of the report and, providing you are happy with it, you will sign it. To counter the possibility of bias a further social worker will come to see you towards the end of the study to establish that you are happy with your assessment and that your primary social worker has conducted a thorough and fair study.

Provided all has gone well your case will be heard at the next panel meeting. Your assessor may make a recommendation that you be considered for adoption of a child or children within a particular age range, but it is the panel who will ultimately decide this.

The adoption panel

Adoption panels sit to decide whether a couple or individual should be approved as potential adopters and, separately, it also falls to adoption panels to judge whether adoption is in the best interests of the child and then to make the match between a prospective adopter and a particular child. You will not be matched with a child at this hearing but you will learn whether or not you have been approved so that you can be considered for children in the future.

The panel consists of up to ten professional and lay members, including medical and legal representatives. In recent years the membership of adoption panels has included more people with personal experience of adoption. They make a recommendation about the applicants' suitability to adopt, based on the submissions from the home study, particularly form F.

The panel meetings are usually held twice a month. They are usually held in private, but some panels will invite applicants to attend. If you are applying in Scotland you must be given the opportunity to attend the panel meeting which considers whether you will be approved as an adopter, but not usually the matching panel meeting as details of other parties are discussed at these meetings. If you are not invited to attend, your social worker will attend and put your case and generally a decision is made there and then and you should be notified of the outcome the same day.

If the panel decide not to approve you they must notify you, in writing, giving their reasons and recommendations. You will then have 28 days to make your response. A formal appeals procedure is in place in Scotland but not always in England, Wales or Northern Ireland.

Applicants who are approved as suitable adoptive parents will usually be given an indication of the age of children for whom they will be considered, plus any particular specifications.

This may mean that they have considered the possibility of adopting a child with a particular type of handicap or medical history. Applicants will have explored these possibilities beforehand with assessors. For example, they may be approved to adopt any child from the age of 0–18 months, or 12 months to 5 years.

You may have specified that you would be willing to adopt a child whose birth parents have a history of mental illness, or a known medical condition. Occasionally conditions may be attached to your approval, such as attending antenatal classes or support group meetings. Once you have been approved, Social Services can begin to consider you for any children that might become available in the specified category.

The outcome of the panel meeting

If the panel reject your application, it may be difficult for your social worker to tell you why. Your referees may have said they didn't feel your relationship was strong enough or that your partner is not really supportive of your strong commitment to adoption. Your partner may have a criminal conviction you are not aware of. Your doctor may have said he felt that your lifestyle (through smoking, alcohol, or poor diet) could lead to illness or early death. Ultimately it may be no more than a feeling the panel shared that adoption is not right for you.

Who can say whether they are right or not? It falls to them to make this difficult judgement; they may be wrong, but they must bear the responsibility if an adoption placement breaks down and they may find it hard to specify the exact reasons they felt you might be inappropriate adopters.

There have been well publicized cases of couples turned down by adoption panels for reasons such as being overweight or, in one case, a feeling that a mixed race couple had insufficient experience of racism. Ultimately, there is very little opportunity to contest such findings as adoption panels in England, Wales and Northern Ireland traditionally meet in private.

Hopefully you will receive sympathetic counselling from your social worker and it may be that you understand the reasons why adoption may not be the right path for you and accept the outcome. It is a legal requirement to have a satisfactory home study if you wish to adopt from overseas and so an unsatisfactory home study means that you can progress no further with your desire to adopt whether at home or abroad.

An unsatisfactory home study is particularly difficult to accept. It may be that you mutually reach this conclusion and it is to be hoped that the process has helped you accept that adoption may not be the answer for you. This can happen at any stage up to placement. If you doubt that you can love an adopted child as your own it is never too late to declare it right up to the moment of placement, as has indeed happened on occasion.

Even if your home study report recommends that you are a suitable person or couple to adopt, it is perfectly normal to feel doubt and fear about the prospect of having a child in your life. This is no different for those who are lucky enough to have their own child naturally. If you feel, however, that your doubts are insuperable, discuss them with your social worker who may be able to help you resolve them.

Debbie and Tom

'My sister had been staying with us with her two children when we were told the outcome of our panel, that we were successful. I was terrified! No one had had any sleep as the children had kept us awake and the house was in turmoil. I thought that I would never be able to cope with children of my own! Now I have my own adopted children I realize how different it is when they are your own and how soon that stage is over.'

Once you have been approved, your social worker will give you an indication of the time you may have to wait before a match might be made. If you are hoping to adopt a baby, you can expect a wait of many months or years; if you are hoping to adopt a child with special needs or an older child your wait may be much shorter.

3

Adopting a baby or child under the age of two

Different agencies operate different criteria for managing their waiting lists. While some may award points based on the time spent on the waiting list, the age of the adoptive couple or age of a first adopted child, their first priority is to find the best match. Ideally, if a child becomes available who has a similar background to yours or where it is felt that her particular circumstances might be best served if you were her new parents, then your names will go up to panel along with hers and, usually, two other couples who are also on the waiting list.

The birth mother is allowed to stipulate the kind of family she wants her child to go to; for example, she may want her child to be the only child in a family or the youngest. She may wish the child to be brought up in a family which follows a particular religion or can provide a rural home.

The panel will meet, again in private, and decide what the best match is. They take as their starting position the needs of the child, and they may feel that the child's best interests are served by placing the child with a family from another agency.

If you are being put forward for a particular child you are unlikely to know anything about it until after the panel has made its decision. If you have been successful, your social worker will contact you and tell you a match has been made and give you some information about the child and his circumstances.

Having waited many years for a child it is a great shock to be told there is a child waiting for you. If it is a small baby you will usually go to visit the child within the next day or two at his foster home. At this point two social workers are involved, yours and the child's. The child's social worker will provide as much background information about the child and his parents as possible and will answer your questions. You will be given a background to his early life and the circumstances that have led to him being placed for adoption.

You may be told the name of the child's birth parents, if known, but in general you will not have much identifying information about them, unless you meet the birth mother, which occasionally occurs. The child will have a right to know more about his birth parents when he reaches the age of 18. You will be allowed a short time to consider, but once you have decided to proceed, arrangements can be made to bring the child to your home as soon as you are ready. You may be given gifts or photographs from the birth family to keep for the child. Bring toys, cuddlies, clothes, and blankets from the foster home which will be familiar to the baby by both touch, sight and smell so that your home is not too alien for him.

Mandy

'I received a phone call on the Friday evening; it was our social worker saying that she had some news for us. Could she come and see us the next morning? We knew that panels sat on a Friday and that our names were nearing the top of the list so I became very excited. Our social worker said she would talk to us both together but admitted that there was a baby for us. The next day, after we had not slept, we found out that there was a little baby boy of six weeks who had been matched with us. We heard all about him and went to see him on the Monday. We immediately fell for him, I gave him his bottle and he fell asleep in my arms.

'Our social workers asked us to go away and decide whether we felt happy to go ahead and also to think of a name for him as they wanted to register him quickly. Naturally, we didn't have to think about whether we wanted to proceed so we spent the rest of the day rushing about buying nappies, bottles and clothes as we hadn't dared to get too much equipment beforehand in case it never happened.

'If I have one regret it is that I didn't have the time other mothers have to prepare for the arrival of my child. I should have loved to spend time buying a buggy, cot, and clothes. Although I had made some decorations for the nursery (we had been approved to adopt a child up to the age of 18 months), I just didn't know what we might need.

'The next day we went and brought him home. After 11 years of infertility and treatment and waiting, our little boy

Andrew arrived after five days' notice, and changed our lives for ever.'

Social workers will usually arrange to visit you in the next few days or weeks, but until the formal court hearing to finalize the adoption you are just like any family who has brought home a new baby. The advantage with this child is that he comes with a set of instructions, having been cared for by an experienced foster mother who will give you a written list outlining the baby's habits, likes and dislikes. Very often adopted babies settle in very quickly and easily because they have been in experienced and loving families from the start.

For a slightly older child who may be more aware of her surroundings, it is much more likely that your introduction will be a gradual process, involving several visits to the foster home and then the child visiting you in your home. Social workers will be keen to make the permanent placement within a couple of weeks.

The transition from foster parents to adopters

It is important to understand that, no matter how old your child is when you adopt her, there has been a separation from both her birth mother and now her foster carer. It is still the law in this country that babies are placed in foster care before an adoption placement is made. Many would argue that, if it is known that a baby is more than likely to be placed for adoption, she might as well be united with the adoptive parents as soon as possible after birth to minimize the stress. The counter argument to this is that the birth mother may change her mind about placing her baby for adoption and then the couple will lose their baby if she returns to the birth mother, or if the adoption breaks down for any other reason.

From the child's point of view, however, this could still happen: the child is still placed with one family, i.e. the foster family, only to be separated when it goes on to adoption or back to the birth mother. If the number of placements were reduced it would surely be to the benefit of the child. The main reason against placing the baby with the potential adopters from the outset is probably because Social Services fear that the adopters will have bonded so completely with the baby that they would resist strongly any attempt to return the baby to its mother.

When you are first introduced to your child you will have many feelings, not least panic and shock. Your attentions will be focussed entirely on the child, but there is one issue which you need to address at this time. It is important to get as much background information as possible about your child from foster carers and social workers. What has been his experience to date? Very often the paperwork giving adoption details is completed many months, in some cases years later, when the information is less fresh.

Frequently there are inconsistencies and downright errors in the information you get. For most adoptions, your child will only have one letter from a social worker to fill in his background until he seeks to trace his parents, if he does, at the age of at least 18 years. Get as much information as you can, however unimportant it may seem at this stage, while it is still fresh in the minds of carers and social workers.

Many children who are adopted build up an image of their birth mother, but if they have never known her it may be far from reality. Any pieces of the jigsaw that make up the child's picture of herself and her place in the world will be extremely important to her and to you.

Now is the time to find out from social workers all you can about the birth family. How long was your child in hospital when he was born? Did his mother hold him? Did she feed him? Did she leave any letters or messages for him? If not, can she be approached now, by a third party, for information? What is known about the birth father? What did he look like, what build is he? What are his interests and hobbies? Was his hair straight or curly?

Ask foster carers what the child is like. Is he happy? What makes him smile? What makes him upset? You have missed out on important stages of your child's development, and you need to fill in the gaps.

Frances

'I found out that my daughter had never been held or even looked at by her birth mother. The nurses in the hospital had passed her around to be held by staff members when they weren't too busy. She then went to a large foster family, who also passed her around and, although they were very loving, she appeared never to have bonded with any one person in particular. Whether this was the reason that she seemed rather detached and reluctant to be cuddled for a long time afterwards, I will never know.'

Has your child any history of ill health? She may have stayed in hospital for a long period and may have required special care. Try and find out as much as you can about early medical intervention. One mother pointed out that when she tried to find out what had happened to her child, the paediatrician refused to tell her because she had not legally adopted the child, even though a court appearance was pending.

Khali

'My adopted son was born prematurely and had a number of medical problems in the first year of his life, which may or may not affect his future health. I wanted to know what had been done to him, so I went to see the consultant, who refused to discuss my son's care as I was not legally his mother even though he had been living with me for three months!'

You have the right to see the medical records of your child and should contact the Health Records Manager at the hospital concerned, who should be able to assist you. If you had been the parent at the time, you would have been with your child; now you need to know what has happened before.

Don't be afraid to return to the foster carers who have looked after your child to ask questions you may not have thought of before. Make a written note of new information and keep it somewhere safe. The next few years will be busy ones for you and when the time comes to know more, it may be too late if the social worker has moved on.

Janette

'The social worker who acted on behalf of my son didn't write her letter to my son until three years after his placement. She knew she was going to leave the area and wanted to bring all her paperwork up to date before she left. The letter she wrote was full of errors and typing mistakes and some of it didn't tally with what she had told us about the birth father at the time. In one letter she told us that our son's birth father was 6 foot 4 inches and in another she said he was 6 feet 11 inches! I asked her to clarify this as I felt this was very important information for my son, but she wasn't able to contact the birth father and only ascertained from the mother that he was very tall.'

You would naturally have an interest in how your child is likely to develop and physical characteristics may give useful pointers to what can be reasonably expected in terms of growth, aptitude and development. Many adopted children have pointed out that they long to know whether a particular skill is an inherited one.

Rachel

'I play music in a band and I would love to know whether any of my birth family were musical. I also feel hurt when people tell me my children resemble one or other member of my husband's family. I don't know whether they have inherited anything from my family as I know nothing about them at all.'

Legally adopting your child

Adoption is a legal process by which a court makes an adoption order transferring all rights and responsibilities for a child from the birth parent to the adoptive parent. Once the order has been made it is permanent and irrevocable. The court will only make the order if it is satisfied that adoption is in the best interests of the child.

Until an adoption order is made, parental responsibility remains with the birth parents unless it is shown that any form of contact with birth parents is not in the interest of the child, in which case the court may remove parental responsibility before the adoption order is made.

The birth mother cannot give her consent to the adoption until the child is at least six weeks old, to allow her time to come to terms with the birth and cope with any emotional upsets which may be caused by the hormonal changes that follow childbirth. She must be provided with counselling support to help her understand both the nature of adoption and what its effects might be on her in the future. If the birth parents are not married but the birth father has obtained parental responsibility through the courts, he must give his written consent to the adoption.

If the birth mother opposes the adoption order she may contest it in court and the court must decide what should happen to the child, basing its decision on the findings of the local authority. The court, on hearing from all parties, may be minded to grant an adoption order without the consent of the birth parents.

Child adoption proceedings are conducted with the Family Division of the courts, which sit in private session to protect the interests of the children concerned. Courts may appoint a Guardian ad Litem for a child, where appropriate. This is a person, usually a social worker, who is employed by the local authority to act on behalf of the child, finding out the feelings of the child with regard to adoption and expressing them to the courts on the child's behalf. If the child, through the Guardian ad Litem, expresses a wish not to proceed with the adoption and the court judges that the child is old enough to understand, then the court is unlikely to make the adoption order.

As part of the adoption hearing the court will want to see the adoption agency's care plan for the child, so that the judge can decide whether or not the proposed plan is in the best interests of the child. If the child has any specific medical or educational needs these may be stipulated in order to ensure that the child will continue to receive the necessary care with the new family.

The courts may also grant a contact order stipulating what contact, if any, there is to be between the adopted child and the birth parents, although in practice this is often left to be mutually agreed between both parties.

The adoption placement cannot be legalized until the child has been in your care for at least three months. Usually the local authority will organize the court hearing and you will be informed of the date and time. It will be a very special day as afterwards you will be the child's legal parent – she will take your surname and inherit from you as if she were your own natural child. It is usually over very quickly; you may be asked a few questions by the judge and then the order will be granted.

If the birth parents are contesting the adoption you will require legal assistance; your adoption agency may be able to help you with this, or you may have to bear the costs yourself. If there is any question of the birth parents contesting the adoption, you should know in advance. Once the court has granted an adoption order it cannot be revoked by the birth family.

The local authority will usually lodge an application with the courts for an adoption order. Unfortunately, there is sometimes an unnecessarily long delay in their doing so – one family in ten has to wait over four years between placement and the granting of an adoption order, and this can be particularly stressful for older children.

4

Children who wait

At any given time, there are approximately 10,000 children in care for whom a home is sought. Some of these children will require temporary foster care while their birth parents are unable to care for them, although this may extend to many years. Some teenagers whose relationship with their family has broken down may be offered a council placement in a Social Services care facility rather than a foster home, until they are legally independent, but the majority are looking for a permanent adoptive placement.

Local authorities have a duty to care for children who are unable to stay with their birth families, and those for whom there is little prospect of reunion need a permanent, caring environment. The greatest resource local authorities have for providing the best care is their adoptive and foster carers. If you have decided that you want to create a home for one or more of the many children who wait then you must not underestimate your importance to Social Services and the duty they have to provide a service for you and your family before, during and after placement.

What kind of children are waiting?

The children who fall into this category may well include healthy babies who, for various reasons, are not easily placed – perhaps because of a history of mental or physical illness in one or both parents, which might, in time, be inherited by the child. Others may be born suffering from the effects of substance abuse during pregnancy, or neglect or physical abuse after birth. Some babies who wait come from an ethnic, cultural or religious background which is not easily matched and some babies have a delay in placement caused by legal difficulties.

Any child over 12 months may fall into the category of 'children who wait'. These may include sibling groups, where some may be affected by physical and mental handicap, and many other children up to teen age with a plethora of problems including abuse and neglect or simply inadequate parenting.

Who can adopt these children?

The criteria for adoption of some of these children who wait are much less stringent than for a baby, in that age, single status, sexual orientation and disability do not serve to eliminate applicants from being considered. Social Services are more likely to consider single men and women, older couples, people with disability, gay men and lesbians as suitable adopters. Applicants for children who wait, however, will find the assessment process as exhaustive and exacting as it is for any other potential adopter.

It is important that the same checks and balances are used as in baby adoption. In many ways the requirements for those who seek to adopt children who have suffered not only the trauma of separation from their birth parents, but possible abuse and subsequent separations from siblings and/or other carers should be even more exacting. You will need strength, health and a good sense of humour as well as a strong support network to take on a child whose behaviour may prove to be very challenging or whose physical needs may be considerable.

Jane and Philip

'We didn't get married until we were both well into our thirties and we had made a positive decision not to have any children of our own. I was adopted and I knew that there were many children who needed a home and so we decided to adopt. We now have three children between five and ten who are all very different and although things haven't always been easy, we have never regretted it for a moment.'

There is still a lot of reluctance to consider white individuals and couples as prospective adopters for black and mixed-race infants and this often leads to such children being moved from carer to carer while a suitable match is sought. There is some evidence that black children brought up in a white family lose a sense of their own cultural background. They may not get an opportunity to learn about their own ancestral culture and language and cannot share the difficulties that racism brings with their adoptive parents. This is why black and mixed-race children, for whom an adoptive placement with parents from a similar background is sought, may be placed in long term foster care with a white foster family without legal adoption becoming an option.

Couples who have older children or a grown-up family have much to offer. It is not vital that you have a high income or own your own home or that you are in employment, but you do need to have a suitable home to bring a child into.

Social Services will endeavour, in the first place, to find a home within their own authority for all the children they are trying to place with a view to adoption or fostering. The exception to this is children whose best interests would be served by being placed at some distance from their birth families. Children who do not find a home within the local authority may be advertised nationally through *Be My Parent*, or Adoption UK's 'Children Who Wait'. Occasionally Social Services will advertise in the local press and there have even been television programmes showing children available for adoption.

Recent research has shown that the average age of children advertised is around eight to nine years. Just over 15 per cent of the children had serious disability or health problems and a quarter had moderate learning difficulties. Of the children aged under four years, over half had a serious health problem or disability. One in four of the children advertised were sibling groups, and 8 per cent were in groups of three or more siblings. Many of the statements accompanying the adverts for single children stated that Social Services were looking to place them as either an only child or the youngest child in a family.

The majority of agencies are seeking a permanent placement rather than long term foster care, and over a third of children are expected to have some form of direct contact with birth families. Nearly all would be expected to have indirect contact of some form. Some of the children would be free for adoption while some may be subject to a court order, which means that the parents may be contesting the placement. In general, social workers do not place a child for adoption if they do not expect the court order to be granted in the interests of the child's welfare.

While every effort should be made to keep brothers and sisters together, there are many children who are separated from their siblings through fostering and adoption and require contact with each other. The level of post-adoption support that is available varies throughout the country, but should you decide to approach an agency regarding a particular child it is important to ask what facilities they have to support you with contact issues, and indeed any other issues, following placement.

It is important for some children to be placed away from their original birthplace, either to protect them from accidental contact with birth parents or to remove them from an environment where they feel or may be at risk.

There can be serious delays in the adoption process, as the search for the right child is delayed while Social Service departments look within their own region, while children in other areas may have been suitable.

As a result of the parenting some children have received in the past many may have disturbing or challenging behaviour, showing immaturity or acting much older than they are. Children who have been sexually abused may act in a sexually provocative manner with you and other family members and this is something you must take into account if you have other children at home.

Children with special needs

Children may have a physical handicap, special educational needs or a history of abuse. For some there may be no clear defining line between a learning difficulty and physical disability; both may result from the type of parenting a child has received or from an event prior to or at birth.

A child with special needs may expect just as much in life as any other child. With the right parenting such a child may reach developmental milestones easily, even when his birth family may not have been able to provide the stimulus, commitment, or support for him to overcome his difficulties.

Georgina[1]

'Two years ago I was sitting on a train on my way to London knowing that when I got off at the other end my life would be changed for ever . . . and it was!

'At 38 years old, single and with nearly 20 years' childcare experience behind me, I had approached an adoption agency, Families for Children, and was asked to come along for an initial interview. I was given an application form to begin the process and, once the references and police and medical checks were out of the way, which took about two months, my assessment began. My social worker was introduced to me at a preparation course for prospective adopters and put me at my ease straight away. My assessment was quick and painless; it took about five months and I actually enjoyed it. I never felt I was being made to jump through hoops or had to give the "right answers". It felt like we were just chatting most of the time. I was approved to adopt a child up to the age of eight years in July 1995, eight months after my initial interview.

'I saw David in the August edition of *Adoption UK*. He was just five years old, with blond hair and blue eyes and about to start mainstream school, with classroom support. I spoke to his social worker who was interested in me and details were exchanged.

'I was one of three families who were followed up, and was visited and interviewed by his social worker and the officer in charge of the small children's unit he lived in. This happened in October. I then had to wait about six weeks for the 'matching meeting' to take place. In December I found out I had been chosen! I immediately rang my friend who told me to come round as she had the champagne on ice, and along with her husband we drank a toast to David, my future son.

'It was decided to leave the introductions until after Christmas. I then went to spend a week with David and brought him back with me. The last two years have been wonderful. We've both sailed through it and things have certainly been much easier than I could ever have imagined. Being a mum is everything I thought it would be and more. David is a happy, healthy and handsome boy. He still has help at school and has had some problems there, but nothing serious.

'The adoption went through in May that year, and I named a star after him to mark the occasion and the legal use of his new name, although he used this from day one.

'Throughout it all I was supported by my social worker if and when I needed it and I was also put in touch with another single adopter who had adopted a child the same age as David. We have great fun swapping stories.

'I was approved to adopt my second child in May 1997, one

43

month before David's eighth birthday. David and I were both very excited. I was visited almost straight away about a two-year-old girl who was featured in *Adoption UK*, but decided, after seeing a video of her, not to take it any further as both I and my social worker thought she had too many problems.

'Over the next few months I had five appointments for visits regarding different children – all boys between one and two years. The fourth of these visits was for Jamie. I just knew he was the one and so I cancelled the fifth visit. Then I had to wait six weeks for the matching panel as his social worker was off work. The panel met on 25 November and I was chosen, but it was decided not to go ahead with the placement until January. It seemed like forever. I did get to see him for a short time after the planning meeting at the beginning of December and was able to ring his foster parents regularly.

'The introduction went well. David and I stayed in bed and breakfast accommodation just around the corner from the foster parents and we spent all week with him. We travelled home the day before Jamie and his foster mum so they could have time to say their goodbyes. The following day I had a call to say he was sick and couldn't travel! This was terrible as we had waited three months for that day; fortunately we only had to wait an extra day.

'Jamie settled in quickly and has surprised everyone by sleeping for two hours every day and at least 12 at night – I'd been told he had chronic sleep problems and had never slept longer than an hour! I'm extremely pleased he does sleep well – it must be the sea air!

'He is a happy, confident and bright two-year-old and I feel blessed to have been chosen for him. He adores his big brother who, in turn, is very proud of him and pushes the buggy everywhere. In fact, two of David's main requirements when I was going through the assessment were that he wanted the child to be young enough to go in a buggy and the buggy must have swivel wheels. I managed to fulfil both!

'Three months later I applied for the adoption papers and the court hearing was the following summer. Now, a year later, I'm about to start the process again to adopt another!'

Other children may have very clear medical conditions which will affect their lives permanently, such as Down's syndrome or cerebral palsy. Some parents faced with such a child feel that they cannot offer the care needed and place the baby for adoption at an early age. This kind of placement is often very open, involving regular contact through visits.

Children with severe and life-threatening conditions may be placed by their birth family into some form of residential care because the care the child requires cannot be provided at home. A small number of these children may be made available either for long-term fostering or for adoption.

Janet

'I am now in my late forties and, until seven years ago when I fostered Nikki, I had spent almost all my working life in children's homes. I'd thought about fostering in the past but dismissed the idea because I felt that for a single person the responsibility would be too great.

'In the home where I worked there were two disabled girls. One of them was Nikki, who has a fairly rare genetic condition which meant that she had severe learning difficulties as well as a physical disability. Pretty soon I found myself "falling in love" with her. Nikki is mute and spent long periods in an armchair or on the floor alone sucking her thumb – initially her vulnerability and her silence drew me to her.

'As life in the children's home presented new demands which I felt less able to cope with, I thought about fostering Nikki and when I put my proposal to the manager and to Social Services it was received eagerly. Nikki's parents, however, took a lot longer to agree and initially said no. By this time, however, the idea of offering a long-term placement to a disabled child was firmly established in my mind and heart so I pursued other agencies. For the next two years, although adoption was talked about, I wasn't linked to a specific child. Eventually, due to a change in their circumstances, Nikki's parents agreed that I could take her on. By this time I was working elsewhere but I began some sessional work in the home with Nikki to rebuild our relationship.

'The council rehoused me and finally, at the physical age of ten and the mental age of about one, Nikki came to live with me. I can honestly say that I've benefited from the relationship as much as she has. I feel that she has enriched my life. She has contact with her natural family a few times a year when she spends short breaks with them as they live a long way away.

'Nikki requires total care because she can do practically nothing for herself so my life changed totally after I took her on. I am now called upon to do all sorts of things I'd never dreamt I'd have to – and I could write a book about the inside of several NHS hospitals! Despite the restrictions such a disabled person puts on my life, and the fact that I can't make plans because her health and sleep patterns are so uncertain and because of the difficulties involved in taking her into other people's homes and many public buildings, I have never regretted my decision to foster her.

'We have two social workers involved because we don't live in the financing county, so with physiotherapists, occupational therapists, nurses, doctors, health workers, agency cover and the school we have a great amount of involvement with other professionals. Together they make sure we get all we need to enable life to run as smoothly as possible.

'Although Nikki's condition isn't necessarily degenerative, there is always the possibility that she could die at a young age, so fairly early on I had to come to terms with that. She will, however, need care for the remainder of her life and I'm committed to continuing that care as long as I'm physically able to.

'My family have accepted Nikki as part of our family despite the adjustments that has involved and she's welcomed by my friends and my church too. Others, like me, feel that we can learn a lot from her.

'When I set out on my adult life with my hopes and plans I hadn't imagined that it would follow the route it has, but I have no regrets and wouldn't want to change a thing.'

Older children and sibling groups

Much more difficult to place are the sibling groups of up to four or five children who may have been removed from their birth families with a view to permanent placement. It is extremely hard to find a family or individual who is prepared to take on such a handful from both a practical and an emotional point of view, and this often results in the children being split up.

Older children, whether part of a larger sibling group or not, may have had a variety of experiences, which may include frequent changes of carer, negligent care, or a combination of both. There are many, many such children and it is extremely difficult to find secure, permanent homes for them, in particular because their behaviour can be very challenging. The contact which many of these children have with birth families may also make potential adopters feel uncomfortable.

Paula and Alan

'Our first attempt to adopt was a nightmare. We applied to adopt in 1989 and our processing took about a year to complete. Six months after that we were linked with five-year-old twin girls and we were over the moon. After a delay of about three months it was discovered that the legal steps required to free the girls for adoption had been overlooked and we were asked if we would like to wait. With hindsight we should have said "No", as the girls' social workers were already showing complete incompetence, but we made the decision to wait, more with our hearts than our heads. We waited some nine months and eventually the match was approved and we met the girls. There followed five weeks of introductions with two weekend stays and we were thrilled with the way things were going. The day after we took the children to see their new grandma for the first time we were told 'The placement is off'. No explanation was ever given and we were absolutely devastated. We never saw the twins again.

'We then launched a campaign to get justice for ourselves and the girls. We eventually won a complaint hearing against the local authority and an apology. It was stipulated that an independent social worker would assess whether it was feasible for the children to be reunited with us. It took this lady six months to decide that introductions should continue. The response of the local authority to this was that we would be "considered alongside other couples". We then made what was the hardest decision we will ever have to make and that was to withdraw our application to adopt the girls. We knew that the local authority was waiting to pull the mat on us again.

'At this point we nearly decided not to adopt and our social worker, sensing this, encouraged us to look at other children. She approached us about another three children and assured us that the local authority concerned were competent and easy to deal with. This time, from first showing interest to placement took some five months. With hindsight this was too quick for us, as we had not emotionally recovered from the previous placement. This meant that we were not able to enjoy the preparations for our three children as our thoughts were full of sadness for the children we had lost.

'The feelings of bitterness and sadness have gradually lessened over the years and we are now busy with the reality of caring for three kids. We love the children very much but the placement has sadly been very problematic. Our middle child, Paul, who is now aged ten, has been diagnosed as autistic – some four years after placement with us. When we adopted him we were assured that his only health issues were common colds and glue ear! We were not told that he had been repeatedly investigated for delay, particularly in the area of language and communication. We feel bitter that we did not know we were adopting a child with special needs which we felt ill equipped to deal with. At the time of placement the children's health records were not made available to us and we were too naïve to question this.'

If you feel you would like to explore the possibility of adopting a child with special needs you will find that waiting lists are less of an issue. As there are so many children waiting, once you have been approved social workers will be keen to match you with the appropriate child or children as soon as possible. Initially they will be looking at a temporary placement with a view to adoption in the long term.

There are funds available to provide support during placement for many of these children. This is called an adoption allowance and is a sum of money agreed between the local authority or placing agency and the adopter. This sum can vary over ensuing years, depending on the needs of the child, so you should check with Social Services regarding any promised financial support – it does sometimes happen that adoption allowances are revoked, although they may remain in place until the child reaches 18 years old.

Beth

'Neil and I adopted Adrian, aged eight, last year. He'd been living with us for a year at that point and we are his fifth family. It took three years from first enquiry to placement. We went via Barnardo's, because of less than satisfactory experiences with our local authority, for whom we had previously fostered for three years.

'I am deaf and wear a hearing aid. I have always managed perfectly well with this plus lip-reading and we have three grown-up children of our own, aged 24, 22, and 14. Despite this, and glowing reports all round, we still encountered obstruction and difficulty from social workers not willing to "risk" using me/us – frustrating to say the least.

'We found Adrian ourselves, having practically no help in this respect from our agency. The problems didn't stop there: after his placement we found out a great deal about him that his social worker hadn't been aware of; for example, he has no lower bowel as a result of a previous operation and he suffered from foetal alcohol syndrome. I remember the very real shock of Adrian actually moving in. When you've only seen small black and white photos and listened to other people describing a child – and having to commit yourselves on that basis alone – actually meeting him and moving him in was a physical shock for both my husband and myself.

'I felt an air of unreality and was unable to get to grips for a while. It had to happen fairly fast as well, which heightened the effect. He has what's described as post-traumatic stress disorder – his basic inner stress level is so high that the slightest additional thing tips it over the top and he can't cope. It affects his ability to concentrate at school and so on.

'It took us three years to get this recognized and the current therapy under way. We were granted a full adoption allowance as our income is very low and it was acknowledged at the time that Adrian would be a child with ongoing needs – very true – the stress level thing has financial repercussions (replacing items broken in temper outbreaks, possessions lost all over the place due to lack of concentration, and so on).

'On the plus side his council pay us an adoption allowance and are also funding long-term psychotherapy to sort the effects of their past bungling in his placements, but we also had the additional hassle that the authority that granted the original allowance has since been swallowed up by another one and they have had a cost cutting exercise and arbitrarily halved the allowance – just as secondary school comes up on the horizon.

'We wouldn't swap him. Underneath it all is a lovely boy with an awareness and perception in many ways deeper than most others of people's problems – he really feels for the underdog and is growing into a very caring person because of it all.'

Through *Be My Parent* or local Social Services advertising, you may have identified a particular child for whom you are keen to be considered as an adoptive parent. This may reduce waiting times although it does not always follow that you will end up adopting that particular child. If you have already been approved as an adopter the process may be remarkably swift. If, however, you have identified a child who interests you before approval, there is a risk that the child may already have found a family before you are approved. Some agencies may prefer applicants who have been approved and who live in their catchment area to those who have already been approved by another agency.

An experience some potential adopters have found is that, once they are approved for adoption of a child or children within a specific age range, social workers approach them with children whose profile does not match. If the age or background of the children about whom you are approached is considerably at odds with your expectations you would be well advised to consider very carefully before deciding to proceed.

Heather and Jim

'We had given up all hope of having our own child after years of fertility treatment when we decided to go for adoption. As we were both over 30 we knew we would not be able to adopt a baby but we were delighted when we were approved to adopt up to two children between 18 and 36 months of age. After a few months we were approached by our social worker about a little boy of six. We didn't feel we could say no in case we wouldn't get another chance so we said yes and after a few weeks introduction Colin came to live with us.

'From the start things were difficult. We didn't really know much about the local schools but he had already started school so we had to find one quickly. In retrospect we should have looked for a more appropriate school for him than the one we chose. It was a small village school where children from two years were together in one classroom and there wasn't a lot of provision for special needs.

'His behaviour at school was, perhaps not surprisingly, really bad. We didn't really know how to handle him and his behaviour at home was even worse. After a while we decided, with the help of our social worker, to keep him at home for a while so that we could spend more time with him one to one and that he would return to school later.

'We really had no experience of children of this age and couldn't cope with his temper tantrums and deliberate bad behaviour. He didn't want to make any friends and didn't seem to want to be with me and yet was miserable when I wasn't with him. I was a teacher so I thought I would be able to help him but it didn't work out.

'We eventually found him another school but the problems started again and the school told us it was our fault! After another twelve months of struggling with him we eventually decided, with our social worker, that we couldn't go on any longer and he was sent to a special residential school, and we never saw him again.

'We had never got to adopt him and felt so very traumatized by the whole situation that we have decided not to consider another child. We feel now that if we had been given a younger child things might have been so much better for all of us.'

Note
[1] 'Georgina's' story was first published in *Adoption Today* The Quarterly Journal of Adoption UK, No.80, February 1997.

5

Intercountry adoption

If you have decided to look more closely at intercountry adoption this may be for a variety of reasons. Perhaps you are daunted by the waiting lists to adopt a baby or young child in the United Kingdom, or you may be unwilling to adopt an older child or a child with special needs. You may have close contacts in another country where there are known to be children available for adoption, or you may have been moved by the plight of orphaned children from news and television coverage. Many Jewish couples consider overseas adoption as there are so few Jewish children available to adopt in the United Kingdom. A child adopted from overseas can be converted after adoption. There is no evidence to show that it is easier to adopt overseas than in the United Kingdom although age considerations may be less of a restriction.

There can be an enormous difference in many elements of the adoption process encountered overseas. In some countries there may be many children in institutional care for whom an adoptive placement in the United Kingdom is the only chance of a normal family life. For others there may be no formal procedure through which children are made available for adoption, regardless of facilities for their care. First and foremost you must satisfy yourself that adopting such a child is in his or her best interests. If you have already been approved to adopt in the United Kingdom and know that you are on a long waiting list with your local authority, check that your details have been circulated to other authorities before looking abroad. Some local Social Services departments have been found to be very reluctant to inform other authorities about potential adopters within their area, and they may also prove reluctant to allow you to use your report for the purposes of overseas adoption.

Before contemplating adopting a child from another country there are many issues you must consider at the outset. These include financial, racial, and cultural considerations and the amount of time and commitment that may be required before you can bring the child home. In addition to the need of every adopted

52

child to understand about his origins, adoption and personal history, a child adopted from overseas may need and should be provided with a framework to understand and know his own cultural background.

Once you have decided to explore this option further, contact the Overseas Adoption Helpline, formerly a government-organized service, now reliant upon charitable donations and funds raised through publications. Many local authorities and voluntary agencies subscribe to the Overseas Adoption Helpline and work alongside them over intercountry issues.

The Overseas Adoption Helpline organize a one-day consultation course, in London, for people who are considering intercountry adoption, as well as providing several publications including *A Procedural Guide to Intercountry Adoption* (which outlines the practical, procedural and legal processes for intercountry adoption) as well as information packs about many of the countries from which children are adopted. There is a modest charge for these services.

It is best at this stage to explore those countries from where children may be freed for adoption overseas, and decide which is best for you. Maybe you have friends from that country, or some other factor may permit you to share your child's cultural heritage more fully, in time.

In recent years children have been made available for adoption from, among other countries: Russia, Ukraine, Belarus, China, Vietnam, Romania, Latvia, Ecuador, El Salvador, Brazil, Guatemala, Colombia, Costa Rica, the United States, Thailand and India. Adoptions from China constitute the largest number of babies adopted into Britain. Chinese people display an overwhelming preference for male children, and the majority of Chinese babies offered for adoption are female.

There is quite a fund of information about international adoption on the Internet, and in the United States there are regular publications which deal with this subject alone. One bimonthly magazine, *Adoptive Families of America,* features pages of advertisements for intercountry adoption agencies as well as useful articles about the subject.

It is hard to say how much intercountry adoption will cost. However, when travel, accommodation, translation, legal and medical costs are taken into account it can be an expensive business. It is not legal to pay any money to enable an adoption to take place.

The Department of Health estimate that approximately 400 young children or babies are brought into the British Isles for adoption each year. They also believe that up to a quarter of those intending to adopt these children will not have received Department of Health authorization or have undergone a home study. It is a legal requirement to have a home study report before you can consider bringing a child from overseas into the country. This is because the authorities in both the UK and originating countries are seeking assurance that the children will be going to suitable homes. The home study will also help to prepare you for adoption, and many prospective adopters find that it helps them to focus on their own needs and expectations.

A private home study report is not acceptable to the immigration authorities. You will need to go about it in the same way as any prospective adopter by contacting your local Social Services home finding office. Social Services receive requests from potential intercountry adopters throughout the year and may have some backlog, depending on demand in your area. It may be worth contacting one or two which are sufficiently near to home to see who can start the study soonest and how much it will cost.

On average, a home study report takes five or six months and you will usually be charged for it. The agency providing the report will need to know which country you are considering adopting from, as most authorized overseas agencies have specific requirements and procedures which must be met. Do not consider adopting from any country which does not have an officially sanctioned adoption procedure and authorizing body, as there have been instances in several countries of children being kidnapped for adoption or women being paid to provide babies for adoption.

The adoption requirements may be very similar for overseas authorities to the United Kingdom. Your health, your age, and the stability of your relationship will still be important factors in gaining approval. While single people have adopted from overseas, most countries are looking for couples. Upper age limits are not always a crucial limiting factor but some countries may make an upper age stipulation.

The country you have selected will want to satisfy themselves that you have given adequate consideration to the need for a child to understand its cultural background, and a demonstration that you have done so may assist your application. They may permit you to adopt more than one child if they are related and in fact, in this situation, it is much better for the children if they are kept together otherwise they may never be reunited.

They may require a variety of documents including birth and marriage certificates, a statement about infertility if appropriate, employers' references and financial statements. In addition to the home study report you will require police and medical reports and referees' statements.

If Social Services decide that they can approve you as potential adopters from a chosen country they will forward your report along with their recommendation to the Department of Health. The report must be up to date (i.e. within 12 months of issue) or it will need to be updated. The Department of Health will then notify Social Services, usually within 10–14 days, whether or not they can endorse their recommendation. Once the relevant papers have been notarized by the necessary authorities, the Department of Health will review them and, all being well, approve your application. They will issue a certificate to this effect and then you can start your search.

Once you have identified which country you would like to approach for adoption, it is usual to approach their Embassy or Consulate in Britain with your application. There is usually an administrative charge for this which must accompany your application. The Department of Health will then forward your papers to the Embassy, which may arrange translation. Authorities in the country will then consider your application and, in due course, inform you whether or not you have been approved.

If you are successful, the authorities will identify a child to be linked with you, and you will then travel to the country to meet the child. Before setting out, you will need to apply for clearance for the child to gain entry into the United Kingdom upon your return. If all goes well when you meet the child there is likely to be some form of adoption hearing in the originating country granting you full adoption. You will need to see evidence that the child's parent/s have consented to the adoption, but this is only valid if given after the child is six weeks old. If there are no parents you will require proof of their death or a certificate of abandonment. If the child is over seven there will be an interview with him, in which he must state his view and that he understands what the adoption will mean for him.

In countries which are 'designated', adoption orders are recognized under UK law. In 'non-designated' countries you will need to apply to a UK court for full adoption rights. A full list of designated countries is available from the Overseas Adoption Helpline (or Department of Health form RON117), but these include most European Community, Scandinavian and Common-wealth countries.

Once procedures are formally completed you may return with your child and notify Social Services that you intend to adopt under UK law. In general, an adoption order cannot be granted until a child has been living in your home in the United Kingdom for 12 months. You will also need to notify the court in your area that you wish to apply for an adoption order, if adopting from a non-designated country. You can consider adopting another child after you have received an adoption order for the first.

Jackie[1]

'In September 1998 we arrived in Bangkok, suffering from serious lack of sleep and jet lag. We then flew on to Nakorn Sri Thammarat, a small town 60 miles south-east of Phuket on the Thai Eastern seaboard. The drive from the airport to the hotel was a real eye-opener to the differences in cultures. The streets were unkempt and everywhere seemed to have some sort of building work being carried out. The houses were small, dilapidated and, by our standards, very primitive.

'We eventually arrived at the hotel at 5.00 p.m. It was such a beautiful place, like a palace, but there was no time to do anything but dump our bags, brush our hair and return to the bus, which was waiting to take us straight to the orphanage to collect our son. Our nerves were really on edge by this time, and we ended up in a traffic jam and the driver had to turn round and go another way.

'We eventually arrived at the Nakorn Sri Home for Boys at 5.30 p.m. This was it, the moment we had waited for since November 1996 when we started on this incredible journey. By now my legs had turned to jelly and I didn't know how I was going to get out of the bus! I hadn't stopped talking for about ten minutes and the funny thing is I was talking to the driver who didn't understand a word of English!

'We were greeted by a couple of gentlemen who seemed to be caretakers. They spoke in broken English and showed us to an office where we were greeted by a lady called Monthip, whom we had last spoken to from England only three days ago. She was a social worker at the boys' home and had our son in her charge.

'We sat talking for about 15 minutes. We were itching to ask where our son was. At this point Monthip said that she would have to make a phone call to clear the way for us to take our son with us this night. We sat like melting jellies waiting for her to return.

'She returned very quickly to say that she had been successful – we could take him that night and come back the next day to complete the paperwork. At this point I became conscious of another lady at the door, but didn't give it another thought until she moved into the room. In her arms was the most beautiful little boy. My eyes suddenly filled with tears as I realized that this was our son. Neither of us could speak as we fought to regain our composure.

'We were itching to hold him but we had to wait a few more moments as Monthip took our son from the other lady and cuddled him. She started slowly to introduce him to his new mum which was difficult as he had no words yet. He was 18 months old but looked no bigger than a six month old baby. He had big round eyes and beautiful golden skin and long eye lashes.

'We eventually arrived back at the hotel at seven in the evening and after half an hour spent getting to know each other, some food and a bath he went to bed and straight to sleep. We did not hear from him again until half past seven the next morning.

'Three days later we flew back to Bangkok. Our son, Tim, had bonded with us both as if he'd been with us all his life. He had started saying little words and even fetched the nappies himself. The next day we had a meeting with our social worker in Thailand, at the Department of Public Welfare, Child Adoption Centre in Bangkok, to obtain a passport for Tim. We had been in contact with this social worker for the previous nine months, since our paperwork had been sent out.

'The following day was the most stressful of the whole week, when we had our adoption hearing. After a considerable delay in extreme heat with around 25 other couples in a similar situation, it was our turn. We underwent a 15-minute grilling by the six women members of the adoption panel and, by 11.15 a.m., it was all over. Tim could come home with us for good.

'The next day we travelled to the British Embassy to collect Tim's visa. Wendy Lewis, who was in charge of the visa section, was incredibly helpful; she showed an interest in all the families she had helped to adopt and was even collecting photographs of those she had helped. Without her help we would not have been able to process the visa in such a short time.

'We returned to England the next day and, as we drove into our little Close a banner on the house said "Welcome home, Mum, Dad, and Tim!" It was great to be home.

'After just a few weeks Tim settled in as if he had always lived here. People told us before we got Tim that to take a child from a Thai orphanage was just like turning on a light. It's true! Thank you, Tim, for being our son. Thank you also to all those wonderful people who helped us make this wonderful journey.'

You need to gather as much information as you can about the child's history, the family background, the culture, and the environment the child has lived in prior to adoption. You may like to take a video recorder, tape recorder, and camera to record any information you are given by people who have known and worked with your child up until now. Collect any keepsakes you can to help you provide the child with a life story book to treasure as he grows. If he has had a particular toy, item of clothing or blanket try and ensure that you keep it. (Take other items out to give to the orphanage or home as replacements.) He will feel less traumatized when he travels back home with you if he can have around him things which look, feel and smell familiar.

It is vital to obtain photographs of carers, other children he might have been close to, and family members, as well as addresses of those with whom you might be able to exchange information in the future. At the time you meet your child these may be the last things on your mind but your opportunity to return and get the information later may not present itself for many years, by which time much may have changed. Do not rely on the information you were given before travelling out.

If you adopt a child who has already started to understand a few words, you should consider learning some of the language yourself, including songs which you can sing with your child, in his language. Find out what food he likes and what medical care he has received previously. There are a growing number of support groups for families who have adopted a child from a particular country, and getting together with others from a similar background will be helpful for all of you.

While there is a slightly lower rate of breakdown in intercountry adoption, compared with United Kingdom rates, there have been incidents where a child adopted from overseas has been found to bear a serious disability or illness, not identified in the home country. This can cause the adoption to break down some time after the child has come to Britain. If the child is then left in the care of Social Services, he will have lost both his family and his own culture.

When you bring a child home for the first time it is important to get a full medical evaluation and a psychological evaluation, particularly for any child over 24 months. Even if you have good medical records for your child you will need to check that the records are accurate, that the child has been screened for infectious diseases and that the child has received appropriate immunization. Immunization documents can be inaccurate so check with your doctor to confirm that they have been effective.

If there is any indication that the child may have suffered physical injury, such as broken bones or signs of bruising and scar tissue, particularly around the rectal or genital areas, ask your doctor to document these on the medical records. This will not only help with directing future care but will also demonstrate that the injuries occurred prior to the child's arrival in your home.

If you adopt a child who has different features or skin colour, you must be prepared for some degree of attention and possible hostility or discrimination. You must help your child cope with this and allow him contact with others who come from the same country or cultural and ethnic background so that they too can help him establish his cultural identity.

Support after adoption

While there is a legal duty for the government, through Social Services, to provide post-adoption support to all families they have been involved with, whether they actually will provide help for overseas adopters is less clear. In fact, many United Kingdom adopters find post-adoption support hard to get, and limited resources may mean that intercountry adoption is at the back of the queue.

Adoption UK can provide a wealth of support for intercountry adopters, as can the Association for Families who have Adopted from Abroad. A list of support groups and government departments which cover intercountry adoption is given on pages 123–5.

Children whose formative months are spent in an institution

For some years children who have been living in orphanages in Eastern European countries have been, and continue to be, adopted by families from the United Kingdom, the United States, Canada and other western nations in the hope of completing a family. It is very important when considering adopting a child from this background, particularly in the former Soviet bloc countries and the Balkan states, that you seek clear assurance that the relatives of the child concerned have definitely given their consent to the adoption. There have been several cases in the last decade where family members or biological parents have changed their minds about the adoption in later years when their situation has improved, and have sought their child, overturning the adoptive placement in the courts of the country the child has gone to, devastating the child and the adoptive family.

Records containing details of parents may be sketchy; medical and developmental reports may be inaccurate or simply unavailable. In Romania at the beginning of the 1990s following the revolution, many children were adopted overseas before it was realized that some of them were HIV positive – this condition had spread through some orphanages as a result of needle sharing. Inadequate health care also meant that some children had polio or other life-limiting diseases.

Many children who have been institutionalized in their home country may have impaired intellectual, emotional, physical, and social development. In fact some estimates run as high as 90 per cent, but there is some evidence to show that these children, particularly younger children, have a good chance of catching up and reaching their developmental milestones after adoption. Most of these children are considerably below the average height for children of the same age but the majority catch up extremely quickly after adoption.

These children might have had very little auditory or visual stimulation in the institution; if they have heard any voices, they will have been speaking in the child's native language. It is hardly surprising that speech and the development of language suffers when they are removed from that environment to one where they do not understand a word and might not hear a word of their native language from one day to the next.

Experience of children adopted from orphanages in Eastern Europe over the past ten years has shown that nearly all the children were severely affected by the lack of attachment, care and stimulation they received. Many of the children had suffered enormous deprivation, having only their basic needs met and few toys to play with. Researchers have found that most babies and children received no more than about 15 minutes of individual care each day. Sadly, some were also subject to sexual and physical abuse.

Another difficulty arose when the adopted families tried to introduce the children to a balanced diet. Because many had been given no solid food in the orphanage, only bottles of milk or gruel, many had difficulty with hot or textured food.

Depending on how long they have been institutionalized, they may be severely affected, both emotionally and physically, by the deprivations they have suffered. When basic needs are not met a child will try to meet its own needs. This leads to self-destructive behaviour as well as self-stimulation through head banging, hair pulling and rocking from side to side or on all fours forwards and backwards, a familiar feature of the Romanian children which observers called the 'Romanian Rock'.

Studies of post-institutionalized children have shown that, depending on the age at which they were adopted, quite a large number have severely disordered behaviour patterns, including aggression, violent behaviour, inappropriate affection towards strangers, and even autism. In addition to the emotional effects of severe attachment-disordered children, almost two thirds may have difficulty with speech, hearing and subsequently reading.

Not all post-institutionalized children who are adopted have all these difficulties. Some are amazingly resilient and make great strides when placed in a loving environment. Many countries, particularly in the far East, have excellent facilities in their orphanages and the children receive excellent clinical and personal care and do not go on to demonstrate severe behavioural problems after adoption. Others will require a great deal of support, tolerance and love to overcome their problems. By visiting both the country and the orphanage you will be in a position to evaluate the level of care children have access to and make your decision about adoption accordingly.

Eleanor and Mark

'By the time the revolution in Romania happened we were on a list, waiting to be assessed for adoption in the UK. I was then 30 and there seemed to be little opportunity for us to adopt a baby, so we were looking at children with special needs, although we weren't both convinced that this would have been right for us. When we saw images of the children in the orphanages we both felt equal conviction that we wanted to help a child in such desperate need. Although we were told it wasn't possible, we felt that we had nothing to lose so we got on a plane and went out there.

'We hired an interpreter and he took us to Number One Orphanage, where we spoke to the Director who told us that, in principle, there would be no objection to us adopting a child from the orphanage. She told us to go away and get our paperwork in order, take some time to reflect and return in a month's time when she would have selected four children from whom we would have to decide which to adopt. It all seemed unbelievably quick after six years of waiting.

'We hired a Romanian lawyer at that point and then we had to discover just what paperwork we needed. We went back home and commissioned a private home study, for which we had to pay. It was completed quickly and then endorsed by Social Services. We returned five weeks later, to find that the children in Number One Orphanage were no longer available, because they had just realized that a large proportion of the children had contracted AIDS and so they were trying to sort that out.

'We then went to two maternity hospitals where we saw four abandoned babies and were told to choose one, a choice we simply couldn't make. In fact, as it turned out only Holly's mother was prepared to give her consent to adoption, two other mothers were untraceable and the other mother wasn't prepared to give her consent.

'At this point, as I had run out of annual leave, I had to give up my job. I took on legal guardianship of Holly and at eight weeks old I took her back to my hotel with me for the time it took to process the adoption. Looking back, it was a very good time. I was in a small room with Holly, no housework, no other distractions, just the two of us. I interacted with her much more than I would have at home and her need for this was desperate.

'I had hoped to find a second child while we were there, as we knew we couldn't afford to make the return journey too often and we were concerned that a future government might stop adoptions. I went to an orphanage with another woman who was hoping to adopt to see about a particular baby we understood was available for adoption, but when we arrived we found out that he wasn't going to be freed at that time.

'I was quite downhearted as we made to leave when my lawyer called me back and said, "Look at little Christopher." I went to look at this little boy who was jiggling from side to side in his cot at eight months old with the biggest smile on his face. There was a note on the wall above him that said that he was abandoned also, giving a name and address for lawyers to contact the family if they were interested in adoption.

'It took two months for the adoption to be made legal, during which time I had taken Holly home, and so my husband returned to collect Christopher. We had the opportunity to have him stay with friends during those two months and we agonized over this, eventually deciding that we didn't want him to attach to them only to be moved on again some weeks later. In retrospect we regret that decision very much and realize that any attachment would have been beneficial to him compared with nothing, that he would have had better nutrition and he would have been safe against harm.

'Christopher was very shut down when he came home. He cried inconsolably, which may have been grief but we also found out later that he had an ear infection, so he was in a lot of pain. He had only ever been outside once during his life, with aid workers, and so he may also have been frightened by the experience of the journey, the strange places, and the flight.

'He slept very well the first night and indeed afterwards, but during the day he was miserable, crying most of the time for the first few days, before the ear infection was under control. He looked at the lights on the ceiling and would avert his eyes if we tried to make eye contact. He was in a world of his own; he ignored our two big dogs and cat, ignored Holly and never registered any feelings when we entered or left the room. He was interested in toys straight away but he still rocked and banged his head and spent a lot of time examining his hands, each in turn, for long, long periods, sucking his fingers and holding them up to his face. These had been his only "toys" and his only source of occupation.

'About nine months later, he would register some displeasure at someone that he cared about leaving the room and began to recognize other members of our extended family. Some months after this he fell over while I was with a group of other mothers and children and, for the first time, he ran over to me for comfort, a concept he had shown no signs of understanding before, when, if he had hurt himself, he would just lie crying on the floor. Previously if I had tried to pick him up he would have struggled to get away from me; in fact the only time he would permit me to hold him was when he was being given a bottle.

'He wouldn't allow me to stay in the room with him when he was going to sleep and we hadn't realized initially that having a bottle in bed was a sleep cue and a comfort to him and the only way he wanted to settle down to sleep.

'He refused any solid food; he would retch or throw away any food that wasn't completely pureed, not even finger foods. It took four months before he would even swallow some ice cream and it took eighteen months to introduce food with any texture.

'Holly had behaved in some ways that were similar when she was first with me: she wouldn't look at anyone, she looked very anxious, was very colicky and didn't show any signs of recognizing anyone. Our lawyer, who spoke in her native language, used to say the same phrase every morning and one morning she raised her eyebrows in recognition – the first sign that she had recognized anything.

'Some weeks later, when she was about 14 weeks old, I was standing outside the window to our room and I looked through and waved at her and smiled and she smiled back at me. She still wasn't comfortable to look at me for very long and wouldn't look at strangers until she was about five, although now (at nine) she will make eye contact with anyone.

'At four months old she was slow reaching some of her developmental milestones: her weight was low and she couldn't grasp small objects. By six months, however, she had completely caught up. She has gone through school well, while Christopher has been late with everything although he is very bright. He has particular difficulty if he has to listen to something and write it down.

'Holly has always been very self-sufficient and easy-going, almost passive, while Christopher has been extremely challenging; he is aggressive and rude, particularly to me, and he has outbursts from time to time when he cannot cope with his rage. He still has full-blown tantrums even now, at the age of ten. He has regular psychotherapy, which is helping a lot.

'I would advise others to consider whether their support and coping mechanisms are strong enough to withstand the strain of adopting a post-institutionalized child; if in doubt, they should seek to adopt the youngest child possible, and preferably a girl because girls appear to be less vulnerable to trauma. Experience of dealing with challenging children would be invaluable but it is not possible to tell at the outset which children are more likely to have problems; some, despite their early experiences in the same orphanage as others, seem to cope remarkably well, while others just don't.

'We have since been back to Romania and located Christopher's birth mother, whom he has met; this has helped him enormously. We didn't feel this could wait until he was a teenager. She was overwhelmed and thrilled, she has not had another child, which seems to be a common feature because these women don't feel that they deserve another child. She touched and stroked him all the time. I felt very sad that we had to leave her and I would love to rescue her from her hard life. She knows she couldn't care for him even now and she wants for Christopher all the things that she didn't have.

'He used to fantasize about both his birth parents and I never wanted to disillusion him because I felt his fantasies protected him from the reality that his mother didn't keep him. Now he has met her he knows the realities and she hasn't rejected him.'

New parents often want to overwhelm the child with the love they have missed, but one expert suggests that children who come from such an environment should be settled in an environment that very closely mimics the institution. They should have a room of their own with no toys, bland colours and little contact with others. New stimuli can be introduced slowly, bland food continued and contact maintained with only the primary care-givers. Whichever approach is implemented, a great deal of professional support will be needed to integrate such a child into a family unit. Because of the profound difficulties experienced, two special support groups have been set up: the Adopted Romanian Children's Society and PNPIC (Parent Network for the Post Institutionalised Child). For more information about these support groups see pages 124–5.

Note
[1] 'Jackie's' story is abridged from an article by Mike Dalby, published in *Adoption Today* The Quarterly Journal of Adoption UK, No.88, February 1999.

6

After adoption

The effect of adoption on you

You have been working towards adoption for many years before your child is first placed with you. For many people those years have brought the grief of infertility, the knowledge that your family could only be completed through adoption and then the long process of assessment, with all its doubts and uncertainties. When eventually your child is placed with you, your pain and worries are over.

Or are they? Some sources have suggested that over 50 per cent of natural mothers and fathers experience some degree of mild depression, confusion and anxiety following the arrival of a baby. This is not the same as the serious medical condition understood as postnatal depression, and it cannot be simply attributed to hormones when it affects men as well. It is not surprising, then, that these feelings can be experienced by adoptive parents too.

After many years of waiting, the enormous responsibility of caring for a child is overwhelming, particularly if you feel a sense of indebtedness to the birth parents, foster parents and social workers. On top of this is the fact that your child will not be yours legally until your court hearing, which may be many months away.

You may feel a sense of being watched by social workers, health visitors, and friends and family. A stream of well-meaning but intrusive visitors may be the last thing you need at this time, so permit yourself some space to get to know your child. Many adopters find that they feel the need to wash the clothes and toys of the child to make him smell like them. You will be encouraged to bring familiar items from the previous home into your home so that the environment is not completely alien to your child, so you must be sensitive to your child's need to recognize, through touch and smell and sight, some of his familiar possessions.

In fact, one of the difficulties of adoption is that when your child has kept you awake for six nights in succession, your house is a total disaster area and you feel dreadful, you also feel that you can't possibly moan. After all, you have gone to great lengths to have this family, thought of this day for many years, and now here you are miserable and worn out! It will pass and you have as much right as any other mother or father to feel exhausted and emotional, maybe more so.

Use your support system to allow yourself the chance to take a bath, a nap during the day or even an evening out once in a while. If you feel that your child needs you by her side all day long, get a babysitter when she is asleep. You will need your rest too.

Once you get into a regular routine you will find life is easier for you and your child. You won't be able to do everything you want to do but you will find time to do the things you need to do. Put your child first, your family second and everyone else last.

A child over the age of six months may behave in a very challenging manner, and other people may think this is your fault. They need to understand that the child has suffered an immense trauma because of the move and all the previous experiences of his short life. Good friends will offer support at this time, while others may have only unwelcome and inappropriate advice. It will take time for you to understand your child and what his needs are, and he too will need time to learn to love and trust you.

How is your child affected by the events that took place prior to his adoption?

Whether you adopt a baby, an older child, a child with special needs or a sibling group, it is valuable to understand the concepts of normal child development and attachment. In fact these are issues of which any parent should be aware.

You have missed out on some part of your child's natural development, because it has happened in your absence, whether for months or years. Understanding normal child development gives you a benchmark so that you can look at your adopted child and see what part of the puzzle, if any, may be missing.

A child's development begins at conception, and experiences during pregnancy have been shown to affect a baby's brain and nervous system. A mother's anxiety about her pregnancy or concealment of the pregnancy, physical or emotional trauma, drug and alcohol abuse all have implications for the child's subsequent health and well-being.

Attachment

The natural process which we call bonding or attachment, which started in the womb, continues once the child is born. Attachment is defined as a profound and lasting relationship which a child develops with a carer in the first years of life. The success of this relationship deeply influences a child's physical, mental and emotional development and therefore a severance of the bond between a mother and her child, even within a few hours of birth, can have a fundamental and lasting effect on a child.

Researchers have found that a foetus at four months can distinguish the sound of its mother's voice from the voice of a stranger, and that a baby three days old can distinguish the breast and milk of its mother from that of an unfamiliar woman. The effects of separation from the mother or poor or abusive parenting from the primary caregiver can have a lasting effect.

It has been proven that unhealthy attachment may lead to impaired physical, emotional, intellectual and social development and so it should be understood that all adopted children are subject to some degree of failed attachment. It is important to understand also that many children who are not involved in adoption may be subject to failed attachment, due to inadequate parenting during their early lives, and that many of the problems outlined below are not exclusive to adopted children.

When a child is born she has an instinctive strategy which enables her to get the nurturing that she needs – making eye contact with her mother, crying when she needs attention, smiling and responding to touch. The mother also has an instinctive response to her child, programmed through centuries of evolution. She does not need to be taught how to care for her helpless child. She will automatically and willingly meet her child's needs and provide a safe place for her child to experience the world.

When the child has a need – whether she is hungry, wants to be touched, or wants to hear her mother's voice – she will move or make a sound or reach out, or try any other way to gain her mother's attention. If this fails she will become angry and distressed, crying, kicking and waving her arms about. Normally the mother appears and satisfies her needs and this earns her baby's trust.

Through a normal, reciprocal and loving relationship between

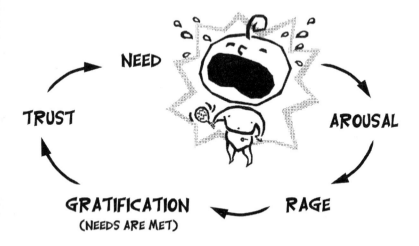

NEED

TRUST

AROUSAL

GRATIFICATION
(NEEDS ARE MET)

RAGE

mother and child, the child finds that her needs are met and she learns that her mother can be trusted and in turn she learns to trust others. She can understand and explore her own environment from the safe anchor point that is her mother. She will develop a balanced personality which can cope with the stresses of life. A child bonds first with her mother, then her father and others in the family. From these bonds a child learns to make new attachments in life with friends, teachers and other important people.

As children we learn to deal with strong emotions like anger and grief from the way our primary carer, maybe mother, father or grandparent, soothes our pain and anger. Calming soothing touch and voice, holding, kissing, or patting hands all help to assuage the fear and anxiety. All these help us to understand that nothing is so frightening that it can't be soothed away. No pain so severe that it won't feel better in time, no situation so aggravating it can't be overcome.

The child who has never learned these simple strategies has no way of dealing with rage and fear and so it becomes a major problem. It takes a great deal of work and a lot of love to build an attachment with such a child.

After birth, factors which interfere with normal attachment are neglect, abuse, pain from illness or medical intervention, and separation from the mother and subsequent care-givers. The child who seeks gratification that is not forthcoming will gratify herself, by rocking, banging her head or another self-destructive action. Ultimately, she will become detached, may fail to eat or sleep well and will become increasingly withdrawn. She may feel unloved and unloveable, a feeling which will permeate all her future experiences. She will learn that the only person she can trust is herself.

As she grows older she may be angry, dishonest and self-centred. She may find it particularly difficult to trust others, will fear any form of closeness and often feel the need to control her environment and those around her. She may be overtly and inappropriately affectionate with anyone, yet it is a shallow and transient affection. Similarly she may exhibit her worst behaviour when at home with a loving family. Other signs of attachment disorder include lying, hyperactivity, destructive behaviour towards herself and others, and abnormal eating and speech patterns.

Such children are extremely difficult to manage within the school system, struggling with their work or behaving anti-socially. There is increasing evidence that, as they enter their teens, children who have experienced abuse and neglect, with resulting attachment disorders, are more likely to be convicted of serious offences.

Some children are remarkably resilient and seem to suffer no lasting ill effects once they are placed in a loving home, but while children affected by a disordered attachment may thrive physi-cally, they may grow up having severe difficulties in making relationships. It is this kind of behavioural difficulty that may lead to adoption breakdown. This rare but heartbreaking consequence of some adoptions usually means that the child is returned to the care of the local authority.

There are many reasons why attachment disorders arise, particularly in high-risk families. Poverty, domestic violence, psychological disorders and substance abuse may be contributing factors, although the disorders are not confined to any one social stratum. Many children brought up in considerable poverty have

71

all the love and support they need. Sadly there is evidence to show that children who received poor maternal care, with resulting attachment disorders, are very likely to become poor parents in due course, so the problem is self-perpetuating.

Sue[1]

'Last year we were happy parents of two adopted children. We always wanted a large family so we were excited when, just six months after our second child joined us, we were informed that the child's birth parents were expecting a baby in six months' time and we were asked if we would be interested in adopting a third child. After some thought we decided to go ahead and over the next few months we were assessed, approved, and waiting for him to arrive.

'It was a strange and difficult time, waiting for "our" baby to be born. A lot of hours were spent thinking about the birth parents. How were they feeling, knowing their baby was going to be removed at birth? We were already deeply attached to the baby and felt helpless, wanting to protect him but having no control over his environment.

'After what seemed an eternity, he was born. On the very day of his birth he was discharged from hospital and placed with a foster family. People asked us why he couldn't come straight to us. We understood that the legal situation was that the parents were not consenting to the adoption and had to have contact, so he couldn't move in until the full care order had been granted and the contact terminated. Those were uneasy months. We still had to wait for the authority that was placing him to take our case before their linking panel. Although it seemed a foregone conclusion, we were still apprehensive. At last everything slotted into place, the linking and care orders were granted and arrangements were made for us to meet our new son for the first time.

'We had spoken to the foster parents, who seemed very nice, experienced carers and had become attached to him in the 12 weeks he had been with them. As he was very young and we had considerable childcare experience, a short intensive introduction was arranged.

'We arrived at the foster home feeling excited and a bit apprehensive. How would the foster parents and their children react to us? How would our other children react? We experienced all the normal worries that go through your head when you are about to meet your new child for the first time.

'The foster family was very welcoming and passed the baby straight to me. He was beautiful. I sat down with him facing me and started to talk to him, but he immediately struggled, became upset and pushed backwards, totally avoiding eye contact. The foster mum said that he did that a lot, as he didn't like facing people, but that he was nosy and liked to be able to look around the room. Once I turned him around so he was facing away from me, he was happier and settled on my lap.

'After all the paperwork was completed, the social workers left and we spent all the day with the foster family. We gave him his bottles and a bath, and found out all about his routine.

'That night I was lying awake wondering about his lack of eye contact and his apparent reluctance to be held. We remembered reading about attachment problems and talking to people who had babies placed with them many years ago at just hours or days old and had gone on to have serious difficulties. We decided that maybe we were reading too much into it and that maybe he was just cautious of new faces.

'When we took him home with us we kept his life as constant as we could. He had his original car seat, clothes and toys. We kept the same bottles and used the same milk.

'The first few days were fine. From birth he had slept in a room on his own but we put him in our room with the cot close to our bed. The first few nights he slept all night, just as his foster parents had said he had. Even in the morning he didn't cry, he was just awake, lying in his cot. He was happy on the floor or in the pram and even when being held upright, but when we cuddled him or gave him his bottle he became agitated and struggled, pushing his head backwards and avoiding eye contact. He would rather stare at the empty corner of the room than look at me when I was feeding him.

'After a few days of this we got out the books and read up on attachment and bonding. We realized that, even though he was so young, and had not been neglected or subjected to lots of moves, he was experiencing attachment problems. After a lot of thought and discussion, we decided that we were going to take positive action. He had to have the opportunity to make one primary attachment and that had to be me, his mum.

'It was not going to be easy, but we decided that, from then on, I would be there to meet his every need, change every nappy, give every feed, bath him, be the face he saw when he went to sleep and the first he saw when he woke. This was quite a challenge, especially with older children to consider.

'In the beginning he just seemed totally detached, but it was only a matter of days before he began to show some emotion. Although we can now see that it was an important turning point, at the time it was very distressing. He would not take a feed even though he was hungry. Every time he needed his bottle I would hold him tightly, in as near a breast-feeding position as possible and gently try to soothe him, singing, stroking and rocking him. Eventually, sometimes after about an hour, he would relax and take his bottle although he would still not look at me, but would look away or close his eyes.

'He started to wake at night, crying. He would still cry and push away from me when I held him, but he cried even harder if I put him down. This could happen many times in the night and during the day also. I was exhausted and my husband was finding it all very difficult. He wanted to help. He wanted to become close to our son and he wanted to help me. If the crying went on and on in the first few weeks, occasionally I would give in and his dad would try and feed him. Sometimes he would accept it but then he would be even worse with me. We soon came to realize that if I neglected to meet even one of his needs he felt I had let him down, and the trust that was beginning to form was broken.

'Even though we are very experienced, confident parents, we felt very vulnerable when talking to our social workers about the problem we were facing. We decided to go to our GP to make sure there was not a medical reason for his distress. Our GP was very thorough and found that, although our baby was physically OK, he had lost some of his infant reflexes and this, along with his reluctance to hold eye contact, was enough for him to refer us to a paediatrician.

'At this time we felt we had hit an all time low. Exhaustion had set in and the contact rejection was beginning to take its toll. It was at this time that we wondered how we would have managed if we hadn't felt so close to him even before he was born. It was a blessing that we loved him so much as, without that bond, I wonder how long we could have gone on.

'After seeing the GP, we decided to tell all to our social workers. We had shared our concerns before, but somehow it's hard to say how difficult it all is. We phoned them and explained the situation. They knew us well enough to realize that if we sounded as low as we did, then things must be very bad. They came the next day and were very supportive. It was hard to see how anyone could help, as it was me who was so exhausted, yet I just knew that I had to keep on meeting our baby's needs. Even to have it all out in the open was a relief and Social Services arranged for some domestic help, which took some of the pressure off.

'The weeks continued and we went through different stages. From being detached he became anxious; the second he realized I wasn't there he screamed and if his dad or anyone else picked him up he got worse. At least he wanted me now even if he still cried. We studied child development books and realized that, although in most areas he was fine, in his social behaviours there were delays. He had never reached up to touch us, to feel my hair, or to pull off my glasses. We encouraged him to touch us, putting his hands on our faces, his fingers in our mouths – all the things that babies usually do when discovering the world around them.

'This summer was spent pacing the garden with him in a front baby carrier; he became comfortable with me holding and carrying him. Towards the end of the summer, life became calmer. He was crying less and had stopped pushing away so much. There were some wonderful moments when he first looked at me while drinking his bottle and when we were singing or playing pat-a-cake. Those months made us realize that we were right to struggle on. The feeling you get when your baby gazes into your eyes is magical.

'Now, nearly a year on, life is almost normal. He only wakes a couple of times at night and loves to be held. He is loving and most of the time he has normal eye contact. However, I am still meeting most of his needs. He has spread his attachment to me around the family and loves to be with his brothers and has a very special relationship with his dad. We have got to the point where I can leave him for a couple of hours with his dad and, so long as he doesn't need me when I'm not there, it has no adverse effect. However, if he gets upset and I'm not there to meet his need, then he regresses for a few days.

'We have tried to work out what caused our son to have these problems, but it's hard to pinpoint just one thing. We think that there were lots of seemingly minor things that happened in his first three months that, when we put it together with the stressful time his birth mother had before he was born, may have led to these problems.

'Although his foster family were lovely people, they had lots of older children and were not actually approved for baby placements. While we initially thought he had a very stable time there, we later found out that the older children took over his care whenever they were home. So, in fact, just as he got used to one person meeting his needs, that person would leave. Some babies may not be affected by this, but we feel that this probably contributed to the problems. He was also put straight into a room on his own, so he got used to being alone. When he was first with us he rarely cried, so perhaps in the large foster home it was hard to hear him cry, and when no one came he stopped crying.

'As we have been going through this difficult time we have talked to many people who have had similar experiences – babies fed in baby chairs and not held, foster parents who do not believe in cuddling the babies because it restricts them, others who purposely remain distant because they feel it will be easier for the baby to move on. All these foster families believe that they are giving the children the best they can, but they do not realize the long-term damage that can be done even to such tiny children by depriving them of the strong bond that any baby needs with one carer if he is to become emotionally secure.

'I acknowledge that our son may have been predisposed to these emotional problems – that it may have been inherited, that his environment may not have had as much impact as we think it did. However, no matter how it came about, he did have the problems and I suspect it will be a long time, if ever, before we can say that they are a thing of the past.

'It is important that adopters, social workers or foster carers are aware of these real problems. They exist and are not caused by adoptive parents' failings. We were fortunate that we had the support of our social workers, but other adopters have not been so lucky. We were also lucky in the support we found through Adoption UK, where there were always people ready to listen and offer support.

'We would say that, no matter how difficult that last year has been, we would not be without our son. I feel that, if anything, the time I have spent with him has made us very close. When he totters across the room towards me, his arms out wide, gazing into my eyes, saying "Mum, Mum, Mum", then the months of exhaustion are swept away and my heart melts.'

A child's development

No child conforms to a fixed pattern of development. They do not all automatically start to crawl at six months or stand at 12. Likewise, their emotional development does not move along preordained lines in a set time scale. Child development is a continuum, changing according to experience, health, personality and environment. A well adjusted child may become a disruptive and angry teenager while a tearaway toddler may grow into a mature and happy adult. The events along the way may shape and alter the finished result and your reactions to these events will have an impact too.

To help your child develop and fulfil her potential it is important to understand normal development and the consequences of disordered and interrupted development. It is advisable to gain this kind of knowledge before your adoptive placement as you will be running hard just to stay in the same place once your child arrives, particularly in the early months and years. Many adoptive mothers report from personal experience that it takes two years at least to start functioning on all cylinders again after adopting a child.

If you are adopting an older child as your first child and you have no children of your own, do not underestimate the very profound shock you will experience. Your life will change in ways you never envisaged. The total responsibility can be overwhelming, the disruption to your everyday habits and your home considerable. At the same time you need to deal with the disruption the child is experiencing, and focus on his needs.

Seek support from Social Services and child psychiatric services, attend courses such as those run by Adoption UK and Barnardo's and read books on child development, particularly those which have been specifically written with adopted children in mind. *First Steps in Parenting the Child Who Hurts* and *Next Steps in Parenting the Child Who Hurts* written by Caroline Archer in conjunction with Adoption UK are recommended (see p. 127).

Linda and Nigel

'I remember a lot of the very real shock of Andrew actually moving in. Both my husband and I felt an air of unreality and were unable to get to grips for a while. It had to happen fairly fast as well, which heightened the effect.

'I had to wash all his – very tatty – clothes with the family fabric conditioner because I couldn't stand the smell of him – very odd, but basic animal reactions were surfacing here. (It worked!)

'Anyway, four years down the line we are now a fairly well integrated family unit, *much* helped by weekly psychotherapy sessions which Andrew now receives to help defuse his deep-seated anger and resentment. Outwardly, and to everyone else, he's charming, polite, quiet, well mannered – but when the stress level overloads, as it frequently does, good old Mum gets the full benefit because he has to let it go and I'm the one he can let go at.

'The psychologist says that he is emotionally aged about three or four (he is now ten) and needs help to grow past it – that being the age at which things went badly wrong for him.'

Changes in care

Children who are placed for adoption after 12 months old are very likely to have been in the hands of a number of different carers. Occasionally a child is placed with foster carers while the birth mother sorts out a problem, perhaps substance abuse, homelessness or difficulties at home. When she is ready the child may return to her until another crisis arises and short term care is sought again. This can happen repeatedly and the quality of parenting skills the mother has acquired for her child may be severely limited. It is small wonder that such a child will suffer considerable problems with attachment and development, as no sooner does he begin to bond with one carer than he is moved on.

One little boy of 18 months had already been in 11 different foster homes during the search for a suitable home for him. This is what one of his foster carers reported:

Ros

'Because he was black and I was white, Social Services wanted to find him a home with black foster carers. He was beginning to walk and talk, and I felt that he was learning to trust me when they decided to move him again. He had already been in nine homes before me and was becoming very difficult to manage. I was heartbroken to see him go as I know he is almost beyond help.'

In hospital, when a baby is known to be going for adoption and the mother has little or no involvement with the baby after birth, maternity ward staff will usually assign a member of staff to carry the baby around with them when possible. This inevitably means that because of patterns of shift working, the baby forms no real bond with any one individual prior to placement with a foster carer.

As there seems no satisfactory solution to the difficulty of obtaining consistent care for a baby destined for adoption, it would seem advisable that potential adopters are lined up as soon as possible so that they can care for the baby from the start. This is unlikely to become Social Services policy however. It is felt that since so many birth mothers change their minds about adoption following the birth of the child, it would cause undue distress to potential adopters when the child was returned to the birth mother.

Alternatively, perhaps birth mothers should be encouraged to care for their baby until placement in foster care. This, however, is likely to increase the distress of the birth mother when she comes to part with her child. Since the child is the one person who has no choices and who is the prime focus of everyone's concern, perhaps it is time the emphasis changed to reflect what is best for the child.

Sometimes the effects of failed or interrupted attachment are not manifest until the child reaches adolescence. It is important not to blame yourself for problem behaviour in your adopted child and to be persistent in your demands for appropriate help and support.

Surprisingly, potential adopters, foster carers, and even social workers are not required to undergo any form of training in child development. To know what can be expected of a child who comes into your life at any stage after birth will arm you with the tools to understand what she may have missed. Most women learn with their children from the day they are born. They mix with others whose children were born around the same time so they can compare notes as they progress. Adopters are not in this position. No matter at what stage you adopt your child, you have already missed a part of their development and you will need to catch up.

If your baby, or young child, does appear to be affected you will need to observe her carefully and try to respond accordingly. If she won't look at you, you can make eye contact with her and talk to her while allowing her the freedom to look where she will; in time she will look at you, perhaps while you are giving her her bottle. If she seems agitated, handle her calmly and gently and ensure that others who hold her do the same. You may want to minimize her contact with too many others at the time you are trying to bond with her.

If she appears not to welcome physical contact, wrap her in a soft blanket but keep her close to you in a baby sling or backpack so that you can get on with jobs you have to do at the same time. Although you may want to cuddle and kiss her, keep your handling gentle, calm and secure. In time she will relax and respond. Keep her environment quiet and stimulation to a minimum. You will begin to recognize the signs that she gives you when she is becoming anxious, excited, or distressed. Learn to respond before her anxiety becomes a full blown crisis.

The effects of failed attachment on older children and those who have been abused

Much research has been carried out on attachment disorder, its effects and management. It includes the withdrawn, sad, and apathetic faces of children in Eastern Europe left tied in cots with no love and no stimulation, and also those whose early care was chaotic, inconsistent, abusive, or neglectful. There is evidence that development of the brain may be affected, as neural pathways are forged in the early days following birth. Children who do not receive the right stimuli may have abnormal frontal lobe activity and high levels of stress hormones which may lead to behavioural and attention deficit disorders.

Where the past history of a child indicates poor maternal bonding or behavioural disorder, there is likely to be some professional psychiatric involvement and hopefully some well documented case notes to help foster carers and subsequent adopters cope best with the child. You will need to have as much information about this as possible.

Child psychologists advise parents to observe their child to see what may be missing. A child's emotional development proceeds in accordance with environment, input, and experience. When development has been halted, input has been inconsistent, and experience has led to mistrust, there is a lot of ground to be made up. This may mean allowing the child to experience some of the childhood he has missed, allowing a ten-year-old access to baby toys, for example, or giving a child something of his own to care for such as a plant or a goldfish. Treat an older child as you would a much younger one, for example by forgiving a misdemeanour as you might with a two-year-old, even if your child is ten.

Understand that such children may lie in an obvious way, just as a toddler standing by the ink-stained carpet with ink all over his clothes and the bottle in his hand may say, 'It wasn't me!' It is asking too much to insist on a child adapting to your home and your expectations; you will have to adapt to the child. It is no good asking a child why he has done something naughty, because he won't know. Children behave in challenging ways because this behaviour gets them the attention they want, or they think that it does.

Gabrielle

'For some reason I was always unable to show much love. I hated hugs, always felt inadequate and not understood. Some people refer to this as an adoptive personality, but I've always added insult to injury by knowing how fortunate I've been and feeling guilty.

'I once stole money out of kids' pockets at school. It might have totalled 14 pence or something, but I can remember writing a note, "To Mum and Dad, thank you so much for having me," and placing it with the money in their bedroom. I fell asleep feeling so good, until the door opened, the light went on, and the interrogation started. I can understand how they felt, but they did not understand me, and my little psychologically unstable bubble burst. I had everything, so why did I cry every night? Why was I terrified of school? Why did I even cross the road if someone came towards me when I was walking to school?

'I'm not sure if I always felt so different being adopted, or whether it grew with adolescence. I was a girl, yet somehow it felt wrong that I was Daddy's little girl. He was quite affectionate and gave me cuddles, while my mum and I just grew further apart. She adored my eldest brother, who was clever and did everything right. (No, the anger never leaves!) My other brother was the baby of the family.

'I used to dream of leaving home. I have a family of my own now but still have quite unstable behaviour at times, bordering on anorexia and alcohol dependency, and I some-times wonder why people think I'm sane.'

It will take time to overcome the resistance and you will need to be flexible, forgiving and tolerant while being firmly in control. The child needs to learn that you are in charge, but that you can be trusted with his emotional and physical well-being. This means allowing him to talk about the things he fears, the greatest of which is the fear that you will reject him as he has been rejected before.

He needs to internalize your values, as he may not have any moral standpoint at all. A child who says, 'My mum would kill me if she knew . . .' understands what is right and what is wrong, whereas a severely unattached child may have no conscience at all and has real difficulty understanding when something is wrong. By showing through your behaviour what is right and what is wrong, and through endorsement of other positive role models, your child can develop a conscience.

Another therapeutic technique some experts suggest is known as holding therapy, where the child is held in the arms of his primary carer(s) while eye contact is made, just as a baby is held by his mother. This has been shown to help increase the emotional and physical bond between carer and child, helping strengthen attachments while allowing the child to express feelings which frighten him, in a safe environment. Sometimes called rage reduction therapy, it also means that the child is restrained when overwhelmed by anger. While he is being held, emotional events may occur between the carer and child that are unlikely to happen while you are just talking. Although a critical emotional outburst may ensue, this may clear the way for the child to make progress in his emotional development.

Most children can overcome these problems, but the earlier in their lives the problems occurred, the more difficult they are to remedy. There are some excellent support services for children who have been affected by experiences prior to their adoption, although most areas have few specific centres. Seek all the help you can, if you feel that your child is affected. Your own adoption agency has a duty to provide post-adoption support, but you must approach them for help as they will not contact you after an adoption order has been made. Local education authorities can put you in touch with educational psychologists and your GP should also be able to refer you and your child to an appropriate specialist. Support groups can also provide invaluable help at this time.

There are several books written about children who have experienced severe attachment problems, in particular *Adopting the Hurt Child* by Gregory Keck (see p. 128).

Education and children with special needs

As the child reaches school age these characteristics may develop further, leading to avoidant behaviour (where she is polite but responds very little to her parents, rarely makes eye contact, and seems busy with other activities). She may feel the need to take control of relationships and become aggressive and argumentative, often exasperating the teacher and fellow pupils and so exacerbating the very situation she so wants to control.

Other children may become more dependent, whining, and helpless. They may be passive and compliant and try hard to be what the carer or teacher wants them to be.

All these responses are examples of the child 'acting out', testing parents, carers and teachers to see if they really are loved and loveable, and in the process making themselves extremely unloveable. This only serves to increase their anxiety and may lead to them becoming so destructive that eventually they destroy the relationships they care most about, in fact the very thing they fear most.

Teachers cannot be expected to understand the traumas a child has been subject to in previous life. With large classes they can ill afford to concentrate on the one or two whose insecurities make them aggressive or manipulative. While some children who act out at home may behave impeccably outside the home, many may be equally difficult at school. It is important to get the teachers on side, without raising issues unnecessarily. This may mean asking a third party such as a social worker to intervene on your behalf to help you assert yourself in order to obtain the right educational support for your child.

Sometimes labelling your child as having 'special educational needs' as a result of his early experiences may help you gain access to additional educational and psychiatric support. If schools prove unhelpful or obstructive, know your rights. Each school should have a copy of *Rights for Children in Education*. There are prescribed protocols for the management of children with special needs. If you feel that you are not getting the care for your child at school that you need, you can ask for support.

There is a lot of controversy over whether children with attachment disorder are more likely to exhibit signs of Attention Deficit Hyperactivity Disorder (ADHD). In all likelihood it is more probable that his early experiences have contributed largely to his behaviour patterns in later life, and appropriate management, without recourse to drug therapy, may go a long way towards improving the situation.

There are, however, a small number of children who have been diagnosed with a variety of behavioural difficulties, such as ADHD. This can be an inherited condition, and if the parents are themselves affected it may render them unable to care for their children. A child manifesting the symptoms of the condition may prove extremely hard to parent, and a recent study concluded that up to 27 per cent of children diagnosed as suffering from ADHD ended up being adopted.

The signs of ADHD, apart from fidgeting, include difficulty in maintaining concentration, in playing quietly, in completing a task, or in following instructions. Affected children may talk excessively, embark on dangerous activities, blurt out answers, constantly interrupt, lose things and seem not to listen.

There are various diet regimes which have been helpful to some children, and there are drug therapies that some parents have found to be particularly helpful. There are varying views about this condition and its management among consultant paediatricians and psychologists, so parents may need to be particularly persistent to obtain appropriate treatment, which some have found to have a very positive effect on their child's behaviour.

If you have adopted an older child who is already at school or about to go to school, research fully your local schools, as some are likely to be better than others at dealing successfully with challenging children. Be honest from the beginning about your expectations of the child's behaviour, as this should help you get the best support at the outset.

Adopting the traumatized child

What does all this imply for the adoptive parent? Is the damage irreparable?

Social workers may not look for, or expect to find, attachment disorder in a baby or young infant who is placed for adoption early. However, if you accept that babies as young as a few weeks old can be subject to attachment disorder then it follows that any child that becomes available for adoption is likely to be affected to some degree or another, although this may not be immediately apparent.

If your experience of young children and babies is minimal,

you are unlikely to know whether their behaviour is something which you need to be concerned about.

Vivien

'I never realized that separation may have accounted for the way my first daughter behaved. As she was so tiny, just eight weeks old when we adopted her, I was told that she would be just like any other newborn baby. Although she was easy to care for, slept well and fed well, she never smiled or reacted to me. As she grew older she was very aggressive towards other children. She seemed so angry. She would stare at people, not hostile but not friendly, and she didn't seem too fussed if I was there or not.

'She wanted to be in control all the time, with me and with her friends. She would become really unreasonable and when I tried to reason with her she would become angry and would break things and smash up her room. This made me angry and I would end up smacking her and then I'd feel so guilty. Strangely enough this was the only thing that seemed to work.

'I felt sad because night after night, when she was a toddler, I would go to bed exhausted and guilty because I hadn't been able to manage her anger successfully and we'd ended up shouting at each other. It wasn't what I expected from parenthood.

'Her self-esteem when she started school was low and she underachieved and misbehaved. She has calmed down significantly now she is older (11) and I asked her recently why she thought she used to be such an angry child. I was astonished when she said, "Perhaps it's because my mother left me." This was something I had never really explored with her before, although she has always known she is adopted. Since she said this she has calmed down immeasurably and is a lot happier. It's almost as if she's been able to express feelings she never really knew how to put into words before and having said it she can accept it.

'When I adopted my second child, he was over 12 months old and really had every right to be angry or distressed, based on his previous experience. Although he was quite distressed in the first few weeks, he was loving and happy all the time. I've rarely shouted at him and never smacked him.

86

'In retrospect I wish I could have understood that my first child was responding to her separation. I'm sure I could have managed her better. I'm glad I've had the opportunity to experience both sides and now my daughter seems to have resolved her feelings she is a wonderful and gentle girl with only very occasional glimpses of the angry little child she used to be.'

Some babies are remarkably resilient and manifest no real problems throughout their life. Others may give cause for concern within days of placement, being irritable and distressed and either under-responsive or over-responsive to touch and other stimuli.

Health visitors, GPs and paediatricians should be able to give guidance, but some may initially feel that you are being oversensitive and neurotic. It is important to recognize that the child cannot help his behaviour. He has not had a normal pattern to fashion his view of the world and where he stands in it. His instinctive strategies have shown him that this way his needs may be met, this way he survives.

There is a severe shortage of good foster care and there is no requirement for foster carers to receive formal training in child care. It is for this reason that your child may have known several carers before being placed with you. Without doubt, being moved from home to home and carer to carer has a negative impact on even the youngest child, and you cannot expect such a child to bond with you when his experience has shown him that as soon as he begins to connect with a carer he is moved on. Where he might have spent more time with one family you may like to keep contact so that he can retain a connection with someone from his past who has not disappeared.

As soon as the child comes to you, you can begin to redress the balance, showing consistent, loving care. You will need to make the child the centre of your attention but not to the exclusion of other family members. Although you may want to keep a child with you most of the time, particularly a baby, you cannot spend every waking hour trying to cuddle him or provide him with constant stimulation; you will both need to switch off from time to time. You may want to put him in a sling so that he is close to you while you can get on with other things.

You cannot be a perfect mother. There is no such thing. You

will need a break from time to time and, if this is your first child, you must not underestimate the shock that both of you have encountered. Most women get up to nine months to prepare for the arrival of their first child, but you may have had only a few weeks.

If your child is older, then there should be good support systems in place through Social Services or the voluntary agency that made the placement. Take full advantage of all that is on offer: courses, reading materials, and making contact with other adopters and foster carers.

You may have to allow your child to relive his babyhood, treating him as if he was much younger than he is. It is not uncommon for a child to remain incontinent, in which case allow him to use nappies until he is ready to move on. Don't always expect him to 'act his age', although sometimes he may do. Let him have baby food, or baby toys; hold him in your arms like you would a baby. These may be experiences he has never known.

The life story book

The life story book is a scrap book that is made in conjunction with the child, by foster parents, adoptive parents, and social workers. It is a vital document for a child who has been with one or more carers, or who has been placed for adoption over the age of about 18 months, particularly when she has other siblings with whom she may remain in contact.

You can include photographs of homes, other children she might have shared a home with, birth families, foster families, letters and cards from key people as well as words and pictures she has drawn.

This can be brought out whenever she wants to talk about previous experiences. It may be that you want to leave it in her room; or you can keep it somewhere safe, so long as she knows it is her book that she can look at any time she wants to.

Transracial adoption

If you have adopted a child of a different race, cultural background, or colour, whether from overseas or not, there are some issues which you will need to address. While it is important to acknowledge the differences that exist, it is equally important to focus on the similarities between you – your likes and dislikes, interests, talents, and shared values. Encourage your children to value the colour of their skin, their eyes, or their hair without making them feel fundamentally different in other, more important ways. It is important, too, not to allow them, or others, to use their difference as an excuse for unacceptable behaviour or overindulgence.

It is also important to let them see and value the diversity of other people's lives. If they see people from many different cultures as part of their everyday lives, they will not feel so different. It is valuable to get to know other transracial families which are similar to your own and spend time with them. If your child's heritage involves a different language or religion from your own, you should take the opportunity of exposing them to their culture whenever you can through contact with others from the same country or ethnic group and through books, videos, maps, and other positive images. Since this child is now a part of your life you might like to embrace some of his culture, by cooking special dishes, celebrating particular days of significance, and observing religious festivals which might relate to your child's birth culture.

Try to avoid your child being the only different child in the school. Find a school where there are many different children from a variety of backgrounds. This may mean moving to an area where your child will not feel that he stands out, although frequent moves to a new area may strain family members as you try to establish yourself in each new environment.

Stand up against racism, even if it is directed at another child, as it shows your child that you will not tolerate racism and gives him strategies for dealing with it. He may identify himself as part of a group with others of a similar racial background as himself, or may identify with your racial background. If he has a positive image of both groups, valuing them equally and for their own qualities and merits, then his own self-esteem will be strong. If however he has doubts about either group he may be troubled both about his identity and about his rightful place in society.

When a child has been adopted from another country, you may take the opportunity to return from time to time, when possible, so that he can experience his heritage first hand. This may even include a return to his original home or institution.

Occasionally, other people may respond in a way that appears patronizing towards your child when she is obviously different.

Avril

'My daughter, who is black, has lovely, braided hair and several times people have come up to me when they have realized we are together to make some comment about how lovely she is or to stroke her hair. Now she is older she has told me it makes her feel like a puppy. I never know what to say and sometimes feel like patting the other person on the head to let them see how it feels, although I know they mean well really. I just tell them that it makes me feel uncomfortable if they touch her hair and that seems to work.'

Children who have been sexually abused

If you are being asked to consider adopting a child with a history of sexual abuse, there are many issues to consider. The first is that in addition to the trauma of separation from her parents, the child may be preoccupied with sex, and have a tendency to act out sexual behaviour. Children who have been subject to physical or sexual abuse from their primary carers cannot distinguish between this behaviour and the normal behaviour which society finds acceptable, as that may be all they have ever known.

The adoptive family must confront this issue and seek to control and alter the child's behaviour, by bringing the abuse out into the open, rather than behaving as though it had never happened. If a child feels that any issue is too dangerous for discussion then the problem may never be resolved. There are many forms of therapy available which will allow a child to explore such unsettling issues at a distance, through story-telling, music and drama therapy, or even writing it down.

You will need a strong, professional support network to help you deal with the sexually abused child, and good training in management techniques in advance. British Agencies for Adoption and Fostering runs a series of courses aimed at carers and produces several useful books including *The Protectors' Handbook* by Gerrilyn Smith (see p. 128). Barnardo's also provides information and support on this issue.

You must also take into account any other children in your family who may be affected by a sexually aware child coming into the household. A good and loving family who have been well prepared and trained can help restore a child's self-esteem by showing him love and respect and in time help him come to terms with his past experiences.

Adopting a second child

After adopting your first child you may decide to adopt another, or indeed several others. If you already have natural children and you decide to adopt it is important to involve your other children in the process. They will have an adjustment to make, just as much as you will. They may wonder what their new position in the altered family will be. If they have suffered previous separation and loss they may be worried about being usurped by the new child. Find out what their feelings are and put right any misconceptions they may have. They may have a new insight into the circumstances of their own adoption as they see the process in action and strong feelings may arise that have not previously arisen.

Bring a present to other children in the family from the new arrival. Allow them the opportunity to feel involved in the decision-making process about this new child. If they really feel strongly antagonistic maybe this isn't the right move.

Older children, whether adopted or biological, may find themselves acting as the family spokesmen to friends and others, explaining the sudden arrival of this child. If this is the case make sure they feel no resentment about it. You will need to focus a great deal of attention on the new arrival and so must make an extra effort to ensure existing children feel loved and valued at the same time.

The opportunity occasionally presents of adopting a child older than your other children, which may alter the family dynamics quite considerably, putting the child who is presently the oldest further back in the pecking order. If this is going to be a significant problem for him you need to deal with it before placement or even reconsider the placement altogether.

For most adopted children the adoption of a second or third

sibling is a positive and joyous move. They can share their adoption experiences together and divide the responsibility of their adoptive parents between them when they are older, if they choose to.

Note
[1] 'Sue's' story was first published in *Adoption Today* The Quarterly Journal of Adoption UK, No.88, February 1999.

7
Secrets and lies

Not so long ago, couples adopting a baby were encouraged to keep the whole matter secret, not only from family and friends but also from their child. Today it is accepted that adopted children should be told of their origins as soon as possible and you will be asked to give an undertaking to the placing agency that you will tell the child as soon as she is old enough to understand, and as the child grows her questions should be answered as they arise.

In some cases, however, it is apparent that adopters do not tell their children they are adopted. Even though social workers stress the importance of this, it is not compulsory that they play any real part in the lives of families after adoption, so there is no way they can check that their advice is implemented.

There are many reasons why your child should know about his origins aside from the fact that it is a basic human right. From the earliest days with a young baby there are questions that will be asked which will require you to reveal that your child is adopted. Indications of hereditary disease, antenatal history, even simple questions such as 'Who does he take after?' prompt a reply which indicates the fact of adoption. While it isn't necessary to tell a casual acquaintance it is important that a doctor should have all the facts so he can best manage your child's care, and it is vital that your children hear it from you.

As your children grow and see other mothers have babies they will ask, 'Did I come out of your tummy?' so you are forced at an early stage to decide what you are going to say. If you lie at any time you have to remember what you have said, and one lie often compounds another. Similarly lies are no basis for a lifelong relationship with a child. In the past many children have found out by accident. If that happens, they will then wonder what else you have lied about.

Sallie

'I'm not sure if I ever felt any different from the rest of my family. It's easy with hindsight to say I did. One day, when I was about 14, one of my aunties had come to visit just before Christmas. We didn't see her very often and she was getting quite elderly. She was talking about who my brother took after in the family, and when I asked who I took after, she just said "Well, no one, of course." There was a shocked silence. If it hadn't been for the look on my mum's face I probably wouldn't have thought any more about it. It all came out that night.

'I felt terrible. I don't know whether I was more upset about being adopted or about the fact that everyone in my family had lied to me. It was the worst Christmas ever. I've never felt the same about my mum and dad and I've spent a lot of time trying to trace my natural mother since then. Funnily enough when I came to think about it I realized that there had been many things over the years which hadn't quite added up.

'I have felt very confused since then and angry with both my adopted parents and my birth parents.'

Sharing the truth about adoption does not have to extend to everyone you know. There are many people outside the adoption circle who do not understand the process or the motivation of those who seek to adopt. Many adopters feel their heart sink when a well meaning neighbour says 'You are brave,' as if adopting a child is a sacrifice. They cannot be expected to understand that you have chosen to adopt, that this is what you want, not what you have settled for. Families who choose to adopt or foster handicapped children do so because it is a vocation for them. It is what they want to do, and not an act of martyrdom.

Similarly, you do not need to share your child's personal history with anyone other than your child and other children in your family. You must govern what and when your child is told about the circumstances of their placement. Many friends will enquire whether you know anything about the birth parents and it is up to you what you say. On one hand you don't want to imply that there is a dark and terrible secret to hide, but on the other it is none of their business.

If you share too much information with friends who have children who go to school with your adopted child, there is always a chance that they may tell their children something which may be passed on to your child. Furthermore you may be

violating your child's privacy if you give someone else information that you haven't had the chance to share with him.

Friends will automatically assume, if you adopt a baby, that the
mother was very young and will often ask quite intrusive
questions, sometimes in front of your child. Always answer in a
positive manner, as it is surprising what even a young child will
pick up from your tone of voice or body language. You might like
to deflect the question by asking why they have asked such a
personal question.

Gaynor

'I was so pleased about the adoption that I told everyone about
it in our little village. I didn't realize that some of my "friends"
had their own views about the "ideal family". When my little
boy was young he was a bit of a scamp and one friend said
more than once, "I expect it's genetic." I found this really
irritating, but not as bad as when another child said to me when
I adopted my second child, "You got him because his mother
didn't want him." When I asked where he had got that idea
from, he said this first friend's child had told him.

'I don't want any kids taunting my son with that kind of
comment and now I realize that I should have been a bit less
free with my information.'

Good friends may ask you what they should tell their children if
the subject arises. You may like to suggest that your child was
adopted because his own family was unable to care for him in the
way they wanted to so they looked for another family who could
offer a secure home. Advise them that it is your child's concern
and that any information should come from him in the natural
course of events, and not be prompted by other adults. Most
children who have no connection with adoption will not really
understand the concept and are very unlikely to be judgemental.
After all, they have many school friends whose parents are
divorced or caring for them alone.

Accept that some people have a negative view of adoption and,
if your child is hurt by the comments of others, explain to him
that other people probably don't understand much about adoption,
and if they did they wouldn't say such silly things.

If your adopted child has been subject to physical or sexual abuse you may have to extend the circle of those who know to include others who may be responsible for your child at any time. This is not information you would share with friends, unless there is a specific reason for them needing to know, such as your child staying overnight with another family.

Teachers or carers may need to know that your child may act out as a result of previous abuse, partly to protect themselves, but also so that they can deal with the child in the best way. If you do decide to share such information you must request confidentiality and limit the information to what is necessary.

Explaining adoption to your child

It is difficult to find any firm evidence that there is any single, right way to explain adoption to your child, but there is a lot of evidence to demonstrate that it is better that your child knows he is adopted rather than for you to attempt to conceal the fact as was common practice up until twenty or thirty years ago.

The way in which you impart the information about adoption is as important as the words you use. If you feel comfortable with the facts your child will recognize this and respond accordingly. If you express nervousness, sadness, or reserve, this will come across too.

You may like to use a book which describes the adoption process. You may find a story book or fairy tale which allows you to tell the story of your child's adoption history or you may even write your own book about the story of his adoption using photographs and pictures.

Adoption isn't an issue that you will discuss on a single occasion, never to be raised again. The subject will develop as your child matures and understands more. Very often your child will ask a simple question which you can answer simply and honestly and they will be satisfied. At other times this will lead to more questions. Occasionally, despite your very best intentions, your child may ask you an important question in front of a friend or stranger, and although you will want to answer fully and honestly the information is probably not something you want to share with a third party. After all, the information is his information for him to share with others at his own pace.

96

It is best to bring up the word adoption as early as possible. Even though a young child is unlikely to understand it, you will not need to expand on it for a long time and only when it is appropriate. This will mean that, as they grow older, the opportunity to answer any questions they have can arise naturally. It is not something you will need to dwell on or bring up every week or every month, just as it feels right for you and your child. There does not appear to be any received wisdom about when a child should be told; some experts suggest around three or four, others as late as eight or nine; but all are agreed that a child should know before adolescence.

If you tell your child when he is very young, don't worry that he doesn't seem to have understood. It is, after all, a complex concept.

Gaynor

'My son always told people he was a doctor. I was a little puzzled until I realized he meant adopted!'

In time they will find elements of their adoption story painful and confusing but your attitude, showing empathy and care, will help them. If they feel that any topic is too painful for you to discuss they will become alarmed. Never let them feel that it is not a topic for discussion. If the subject is raised at the wrong time, when someone else is there, or you are hurrying for an important meeting, say, 'Why don't we talk about this at bedtime when we have a little more time?' If the meeting can wait, take the time there and then to answer the question.

You may not know the answers to the questions and some are very difficult to answer. There will be many things you don't know, if you haven't met birth parents or have very little information about your child's history. Just admit that you do not know.

There are some things you should take great care not to say, such as, 'We will send you back if you're naughty' or, 'You should be grateful for all we've done for you!' These are the kind of words that natural parents may use any time when scolding their children but, even when angry, be cautious of saying something which may stick in the mind of your child.

When describing the concept of adoption to your child you may like to talk about the time you first heard about them, when you first saw them, and how you felt.

Gaynor

'When I talk about adoption to my child I like to tell him that his birth parents knew that they couldn't look after him, and they wanted the very best life for him, and so they asked Rose (our social worker) to help them find him a mummy and daddy. I told him that we went to see him and that we loved him straight away, and that Rose said, "Would you like this baby to be your baby?" and we said "Yes" and then Rose asked you whether you would like us to be your mummy and daddy and you said "Yes".

'I talk a lot about how he behaved as a baby and how much we loved him. He loves to hear me talk about his early words and some of the things he did. I often tell him how much I love him and that I know his birth parents would be very proud of him too.'

From time to time children will think about their birth parents, what kind of people they are and why they couldn't keep them. It is important sometimes to understand any misconceptions your child might have gathered. If you tell your child that the birth parents loved them very much but couldn't look after them, this may put additional questions in the child's mind: 'Perhaps, since you love me too, if things get difficult you will place me for adoption again.' In fact it is nonsensical to say, 'Your mother loved you so much she gave you away'. Similarly, suggesting that poverty was the reason for adoption may make the child worry that their parents should have been helped more and that if your circumstances changed you might be forced to do the same thing.

Children may sometimes feel guilty and responsible for the adoption and again there is much you can do to reassure them that it was nothing they did, not their behaviour nor their medical condition or disability if they have one. It is important that your child doesn't perceive the adoption process as you saving him; let him know that adoption was a positive move that you sought to form your family – that it fulfilled your need and was not an altruistic gesture.

Unthinking neighbours may say, 'Oh you are good to take on this child, you are brave, I couldn't do it.' It is important to stress that this was a decision you took because the child was very much wanted in your family. If you have a religious faith, you may like to say that your God sent the child to you. Others may say that it was destiny that brought you together.

If infertility is the reason you have chosen to adopt, this may be a very sad subject for you and it is important to let your child know how much you wanted them, not that you were disappointed because you couldn't have your own child.

Children may build up a fantastical picture of their birth parents, which has little bearing on the truth. They may worry that they are dead. You can reassure your child that the birth mother is probably alive and well, but it is useful to have as much information as you can get from your local authority or post-adoption support agency which you can give when the time is right. Remembering all you are told about the child's history at the time you meet them for the first time is impossible, so you might like to take a tape recorder or Dictaphone with you to record the voices of foster carers and social workers.

Of course your child may remember everything about their adoption if they were older at the time of placement or they have had many carers. Again it is important to try to answer their questions honestly, openly, and positively. It is still important to explain the concept of adoption to a child adopted when they are older, to avoid any confusion in their minds about your status. They may feel that they may be taken away from you one day and so it is important to reassure them that you are their mummy and/ or daddy now and you will be theirs for ever.

It is valuable to your child for you to depict the birth parents in a positive light, even if they were inadequate parents. If she believes that one or both of her birth parents were 'bad people' she may feel that she too is bad. If parents were abusive or neglectful it would be preferable to explain that they were unable to look after their child as well as they wanted to and that they wanted a better life for her. It is very important to let the child know that she was not responsible for the breakdown.

It is unwise to bring the subject up yourself too often, once you have established the fact of adoption, but it is important for your child to feel that they can bring it up when they need to and know

SECRETS AND LIES

that you will be open about it. It is never a good idea to bring up
the subject of adoption during a time of family crisis or when you
are angry for some reason. It is also helpful for your child to meet
other adopted children so that they do not feel unique. The
various support bodies and post-adoption support agencies can
put you in contact with other adopters.

It is natural that the concept of adoption may, at some time,
cause your child to feel sad – sad because his mother left him, sad
because you are not his natural mother, and sad because he knows
that his birth mother may be thinking about him and missing him,
just as he is thinking about her. This will alter as your child grows
older and may cause more concern during adolescence. It is
unlikely to persist and should not stop them enjoying a full and
happy life. After all, there are many things in life that can make
us sad but we learn to live with them and not dwell on them.

Just because your child does not discuss the facts of his
adoption doesn't mean that he isn't thinking about it; in some
cases he may even deny it. Birthdays may be particularly painful
and if he is feeling sad it is important to let him acknowledge that
and know that it's all right to talk about his feelings.

When teenage children become angry and challenging, as they
so often do, the fact of adoption may be another weapon to beat
the parents with. He may feel that his birth family would have
been much better than you. It is important to remember that most
adolescents at some time wish that their parents were different,
more accommodating and more tolerant. There is little you can do
other than to continue to let them know you love them, while
keeping the boundaries clear about what you believe is acceptable
behaviour. Adopting a child during his teenage years is particularly difficult for both of you and while there is little to explain
about adoption there is still much to resolve. It may be helpful to
use a third party, whether it is a social worker or therapist.

If there are unpalatable facts, such as your child being born as a
result of incest or rape, these can really only be understood when
the child has reached sufficient maturity, perhaps in the late teens.
In this situation it is best to be matter-of-fact and not condemna-
tory. If the child thinks this is a serious issue they may feel that
this reflects on them. Seek the support of post-adoption counsellors who will be able to help you with issues like this.
Nonetheless, in a matter-of-fact way, even when your child is

100

young, you should give him a vague outline of his history, so that when he is older he does not feel that you have lied or kept from him something too terrible to report.

Your child will understand a great deal if he is involved with the process of adopting a second child, and through this he will understand more about the process you went through to adopt him. It will give him a good opportunity to ask questions about his own history although he might also pick up some misconceptions at the same time.

Molly

'My daughter once told me that she was glad we had adopted her because we are so much younger than her birth parents. As we were over 35 when we adopted her I was quite surprised to hear her say this. When I asked her what made her think that, she said that she thought her birth parents were quite elderly. It turned out that she thought this because the foster parents our second adopted child had been living with until he came to us were in their sixties. She had confused foster parents with birth parents.

'I have tried to explain a few times that her birth parents are considerably younger than we are, but I'm not sure this has sunk in yet.'

One child who failed to attach to his adoptive family revealed later that he thought his adopters had kidnapped him from his birth parents. They, in wanting to protect him, had never told him that his mother was a drug addict who had abandoned him. Both had avoided discussing the issue until the child was six, and they sought therapy to cope with his attachment disorder. It is important to listen to what your child thinks, and also to remember that, while our own life stories are not of overwhelming interest to us because we know the people in our own ancestry, your child's history is overwhelmingly important to him because he has a vacuum before he was adopted.

There are no upper age limits when it comes to answering your child's questions about her adoption. There will still be questions and issues when your child is an adult, possibly when she comes to have a child of her own.

8

Birth families and adopted children

No matter how much you may wish to forget that your adopted child is not your child by birth there will be many times during her life when you will think of her parents. In some cases you may have the opportunity of meeting either the mother or both birth parents at an early stage in the adoption process and possibly at subsequent prearranged meetings. However, it is still relatively uncommon for direct contact to be maintained between adoptive and birth families.

It is unusual, nowadays, for a child, particularly a young child, to become available for adoption against the wishes of the birth mother, unless Social Services found the birth mother to be mentally or physically unable to parent safely. In the past many young girls, finding they were pregnant, felt they had little or no choice about giving up their child in the face of hostility towards single, unmarried mothers. Many of the young children who become available for adoption today, whether British or otherwise, have been relinquished in the reluctant belief that they will have a 'better life' if placed for adoption than they might otherwise have done.

Some birth mothers are subject to enormous pressure from their family, partner, or social circumstances when they discover their pregnancy, forcing them to feel that they have no alternative other than termination of pregnancy or adoption. Many young women who feel that their baby will have a better life if placed for adoption feel tremendous pain at the separation, and in some cases change their minds once the child is born. Others take the view that they do not wish to hold or even look at the baby after birth because they know they will find it impossible to part.

In many cases the mother will deny herself the opportunity to grieve, or family members may avoid the subject, yet she is living with the physical effects of pregnancy and childbirth as well as the hormonal ups and downs that follow. For some a grave effort is made to suppress the enormous guilt and sadness that follows – feelings that may be suppressed for many years.

102

Maxine

'My story starts in 1979 when my family moved from a big city to a small seaside village in Lincolnshire. I was just 15 and very naïve, in a new place with no friends – just my younger sisters. My mother and stepfather had a business to run which left little time for three teenage daughters. I met a local lad a little older than me. He was a bit of a tearaway, but I fell head over heels in love with him and one thing led to another and I ended up pregnant. I never told him about the pregnancy; I didn't want him to get into trouble so I didn't tell anyone he was the father.

'I was sent away to a mother-and-baby home in Nottingham and I had to stay there until after the baby was born, when I could go home, but without the baby. Many family members were not even told and my only visitors were my mum once or twice and my older sister and my social worker.

'The home wasn't too bad. The other girls were nice to me although we didn't keep in touch afterwards. I had a long and difficult labour, but when I saw my daughter I knew instantly I would love her for ever. She was perfect and beautiful and I called her Carla. I spent every moment I was able to with her while I was in the hospital. My mother and stepfather came for me and I thought that when they saw Carla they would change their minds and let me keep her, but they never mentioned her name, ever.

'I had no one to talk to about how I was feeling. I had all these emotions running through me. I had just left my daughter in a hospital and nobody seemed to care that there was a little person who needed me and I needed her. I was just 16 and did as I was told. If I had been as strong then as I am now, then things might have been different.

'The social worker took me to see Carla in the foster home when she was 6 weeks old and I know she knew me. I fed her and spent an hour with her. I wanted so much to keep her but nobody seemed to want to help me. The papers were signed but I can't remember signing them. Years later I found out that the social worker had written to me but I never got the letters. I assume that my stepfather destroyed them.

'I tried to put Carla to the back of my mind and get on with

103

my life, but this was hard to do. I couldn't bear to look at babies with their mums and dads – it would break me up inside. Her birthday and Christmas were the worst times.

'My search for my daughter started in February 1997. I heard about a birth mothers group for others in the same situation which I started going to every month.

'I found out that there was a photograph in my file of Carla, aged nine months; it had been there for 16 years! It was wonderful to have the photo but receiving it was hard, like losing my child all over again. My emotions were upside down. I couldn't eat or sleep. My husband found me very difficult to live with during the two years of my search as I was obsessed, but it was the only way of dealing with all the pain that had been bottled up for so long.

'I went to the records office in London and searched through 18,000 names in the 1980 adoption register, looking for girls with the name Emma, as I remembered the social worker had said the new family were going to call her Emma. I found 40 names and had to send for copies of the birth certificates for each one. I had to send away for a few at a time as they cost £10.50 each but my contact from Norcap got some of them for me as he was able to get them directly for £6.50.

'Each certificate that came back was hard to open as this could be the one that would give me my daughter, but it was not to be. I had to go back to London, and this time write down every girl's name and send for them in number order. It seemed to take forever, every week getting just three or four, I was beginning to think I would never find her, but one Wednesday in June my counsellor from Norcap phoned me to tell me he thought he had the right one at last. I had found my baby and her name was Nina.

'I sat and cried for hours after this call. I was shaking with joy, pleasure, and fear. It was not too difficult to trace her and then Lincoln Social Services contacted Nina's parents with a letter from me. Unfortunately they did not want to hear from me and told me that although Nina knew, and had always known about her adoption she did not want to meet me at this stage.

'I have never felt so low, depressed, and rejected as I did at that time. I now have a four-year-old son whom I love dearly, but I have never stopped loving my daughter. I had to have four years of fertility treatment to have my son and I felt I was being punished for giving up Carla. I miss her so much and want so much to meet her.'

As adoptive parents, you may take the view that the less you think about the birth parents the better. But providing you have been open about adoption with your child, you can guarantee that there will be times when he will be thinking about his birth mother and she will be thinking about him – maybe not every day, but certainly on special days such as Christmas and birthdays.

The current adoption system embroils itself in a web of secrecy. You are unlikely to have more than a sketchy picture of the birth mother, and often there is even less information about the putative father. You are unlikely to meet either parent and any information you receive will come via a social worker. Your child will only learn from the information you provide in the first instance. If the information you received at the time of placement was inaccurate or your state of mind while preparing to welcome your new child into your home was not entirely focussed on the information you were given, who could blame you? If you want to fill in the gaps in later years when you have a little more time to consider the issue you may find the social worker has moved on and the information is scant.

One adoptive mother tells how, when she wanted to fill in some of the gaps for her nine-year-old son, she was informed that the files were lost:

Gaynor

'I wanted to see whether the birth mother would like to know how our son was doing. She is often in his thoughts and mine and I felt that she may like photos and some basic information. My second adopted child has photographs of his birth mother and I don't really want my older child to know this unless I can get a photograph for him. Additionally I would have liked to know if she has married and perhaps had more children so that I can tell my son as he grows up rather than leave a big gap in his life which may or may not be filled later. Why should they have to wait until they are 18 for this type of information?

'When I spoke to my social worker she advised me not to "rock the boat" and then told me the files were missing. He is only nine and so I wonder what chance he has of tracing when he is older. I said I would like a photograph if it were possible but the social worker said that this was inadvisable as he might be able to recognize her from this (we still live in the same area).

'When I pointed out that the social worker who worked with the birth mother had given me the home address from the letter she finally sent four years after placement, explaining the reasons he was placed for adoption, I was advised to blank it out. The only piece of information he will get for the first 18 years of his life and I am supposed to start censoring it!'

Social Services provide counselling support for birth mothers but the response of their own family may be very different, lacking in support, abusive, indifferent, and in some cases acting as if the pregnancy and the child never existed. This may make the birth mother very distressed in both the short and long term and may determine her attitude towards tracing her child one day in the future.

Jennifer

'No written account can possibly illustrate the feelings of a birth mother, the feelings of anger towards society and one's family, the pressure to do the "best thing". I was 19 in 1972 when I became pregnant. All through the pregnancy I felt close to the baby and despite the pain of the labour I can remember one of the nurses saying, "Pull yourself together – you're not keeping this child anyway." When I saw him I had this surge of love and realized I wanted to keep him. I told the social worker I had changed my mind.

'The National Council for Unmarried Mothers found me a place to live in a house with a lot of other single mothers but after eight weeks my savings ran out. My family wouldn't let me return with the baby and it was then I realized I had no option but to let him go. I could have ended up in the gutter, struggling to survive, and I could never do that to a baby. I went out and bought him an outfit so he could look his best and then went back to the social worker.

'I felt that the social worker only saw me as a source of a child for the couple. My feelings didn't come into it. Nobody said, "Are you sure about this?" I was totally on my own. I handed him over with a few bits and pieces, including a bracelet engraved with my name which I hope his adoptive parents gave to him. I was told that they understood the pain it caused me and, in years to come, they would explain to him. I wrote him a letter telling him I loved him and was doing this for him to have a better life and hoped that when he was old enough he would understand he wasn't forgotten, that I would never forget him.

'I have been searching for him since 1992 without success. I want to find him for so many reasons; he may not know he is adopted, but if he does know he may not have been given the right reasons. I cannot go to my grave not knowing what happened to my child who I last saw as an eight week old infant.

'I do not wish to upset anyone or disrupt his life in any way. I just want the chance to explain to him myself the circumstances leading up to his adoption. He may well have a family of his own, I could be a grandmother. Is he alive, is he well, is he happy?

'I thought of him on his first Christmas opening his presents. If only I could have sent him a card or a gift! But I felt invisible. In the so-called adoption "triangle" only two parties matter, the adoptee and the adoptive parents. I bear no malice whatsoever to my son's parents; I am grateful to them for providing him with a home and security. I pray that the placement was a successful one. I will always live with the guilt of giving away my son to strangers.

'I am also preparing myself for rejection. I don't know how I will cope with that – it will be like living the adoption all over again – but at least I'll know. For all these years I have been living in limbo.'

It is difficult to determine how many adopted children seek to find their birth parents or how many would just like more information. It would appear that more adopted girls seek to find birth mothers than boys, particularly when they have their own children. Many adopted children feel that they will hurt their adoptive parents if they seek birth parents, so they leave it until after one or both adoptive parents have died. The danger of this is that the passage of time may mean that the trail has grown cold and contact may never be made; or, even worse, the child may discover that the birth mother has died.

Jenny

'I was adopted 50 years ago at the age of five and the subject of adoption is never far from my mind. I have a friend who has two adopted boys, now adults. We have discussed the subject many times from both sides of the fence. We decided this year to go to Cornwall for a few days and I went to look at the outside of my birth mother's house nearby. It was a nice, cosy feeling to be in the place where I was born and I lapped up the atmosphere. Later, however, my friend started to question the right that I had to search for my birth parents, as people who give up their children do so because they don't want them. I was horrified and very distressed at what she said, not so much for what she had said, because I know that it is not true in all cases, but that she said it at all.

'When I told my son about the incident, he arranged a stay for the two of us in Cornwall in August. As we walked towards the house the door opened and my mother and her husband came out. She was a small, white-haired lady, very smartly dressed, walking with a stick. We followed them for a while trying not to be noticed. She spoke to several people that she knew with a friendly manner. At first neither my son nor I could see any resemblance to myself, until she smiled. I have a toothy smile. Her face was longer than mine, more like my son's in fact, and her nose is like my daughter's, but the smile was mine!

'As to how I felt, it's hard to say. I was not overcome with emotion, just very excited. We walked away. Later when we had calmed down and talked about it, I decided that I felt a great sense of achievement. What I had set out to do all those years ago had happened. I felt absolutely wonderful then and I still do several months later.

'I have a face to put to the person now. The image I had of her through the years has now gone, and I feel as though I have grown up at last.'

Not all adoptive parents feel that they don't want their children to know more about their natural parents.

Gaynor

'I have always been interested to know more about my two boys' natural mothers. I never met either of them and yet I feel I owe them an enormous debt of gratitude for bringing my boys into the world and entrusting them to me, even though they never knew me. They must be very special women because their children are such wonderful boys. They have brought sunshine into my life and I would love their mothers to know how very beautiful and precious they are.

'I have kept a photographic diary of the boys for their mothers should they ever want them and I would be happy to hear from them about their lives and pass back information about the boys. If when they are older the boys want to trace them, I will encourage them. I don't feel threatened by them. After all, I want the boys to grow up to be independent adults and any relationship they have with me then I will have earned. If they don't want to come back home it will be my fault, not their birth mothers'.'

Even if you have never stated as much, your adopted child may feel that to question you too much about her birth family would cause you pain. In time she may want to trace her birth family, or attempts may be made, after she reaches the age of 18, to trace her.

Gill

'I became pregnant at the age of 18, just before I set off to University in London, to fulfil my parents' dreams. I returned after one term to confront my parents with the bitter news and get married. For several reasons the wedding didn't take place and I was left to decide what to do after the birth of the child. It is never an easy decision. My parents were not wealthy and my father was nearly sixty, close to retirement. Mine was a religious family and I certainly felt that I had brought shame on them all by my condition.

'The people who influenced my decision were my parents, the minister and my mother's friends. I can't remember my social worker but there must have been one. I was counselled that I did not have the resources or the right to keep my baby; one parent was only half a family and adoption would provide a better and happier life than I could.

'My daughter Katie was born, and I cared for her during six bittersweet weeks and then said my last goodbye, or so I thought, as the law then required no further contact ever again.

'Life went on. I returned to University because I could think of nothing else to do. I met my husband, fell in love and got married. He knew about Katie. It was then that I wished I had kept her, as this loving man would have welcomed her as his own. I longed for another child, a baby that was mine for ever, but prudence told me to wait until the scars had healed, so it was five years before we decided to start a family. The pregnancy didn't happen. Months of expectancy resulted in disappointment. Was God paying me back?

'We looked into adoption and, when I was 31, Philip was placed with us. The same ongoing problem seemed to mean that we would not have another child so we looked to adoption again but, just as we were approved, I discovered that I was pregnant. My second daughter, Carolyn, was born 16 years after my first. I had been given a second chance to prove myself a fit mother, but what about those other children we knew about who, for no fault of their own, were languishing without caring homes? We were approved adopters. It was relatively easy to find an older child to round out the family, so Daniel, aged eleven, joined us when Carolyn was one and Philip five.

'Those family years were happy, busy years, but not without their trials. Thankfully there was not much time to dwell upon the past, but I still remembered Katie, wondered if she was happy, what she had become, and whether she would ever contact me. The date of her eighteenth birthday passed. I waited on tenterhooks but no letter or phone call came.

'When the law changed I had registered my name on the Adoption Register and with Norcap, so it would be easy for her to trace me. It hurt me that I might pass her in the street and not know that she was my child. I did not feel that I had the right to look for her, and took the fact that she had not contacted me to mean her life was going well.

'Daniel was a quiet child, who had had some sad experiences in life, so we were unprepared for the change in his teenage years when he started staying out all night, refusing to obey the house rules and became the usual rebellious teenager. "It must be because he's adopted," I thought, and Philip's serene passage from child to adult seemed to bear this out. However Carolyn found the voyage much more difficult than either of the boys, which has made me realize how much a child's behaviour is due to basic personality rather than what a parent does or doesn't do. You have to stay with them through the rough times as well as the smooth; that's what being a parent really means. If it was all cuddles and warm companionship, the job would be too easy and it saddens me that adopted parents can easily reject a child during the teenage troubled years when their support is needed most.

'When the letter finally came, my whole world was turned upside down. I cried, I laughed, I phoned my husband at work in an incoherent state, so he assumed something terrible had happened. The social worker, who supervised the meeting with Katie, now called Rachel, was a caring, careful man. We exchanged letters first and what a surprise. There were so many similarities between my first-born daughter and myself, even down to liking the same books and films, having the same job and the same hobbies! Only her interest in cycling did not fit. I was dozing off to sleep with a happy smile on my face when it came to me. Her father had been a speedway cyclist.

'We agreed to meet on neutral territory, in a London hotel. My main fear was that she would not like me. I was desperate to be liked and understood by this important person in my life, whom I had not met for 28 years.

'We met and talked for several hours about the past and how she came to be born and adopted. We went to a gallery, I remember. Neither of us is too demonstrative and we both tried to control our emotions in this public place, but both of us shed a tear. I was in such a daze I got on the wrong bus going home and ended up having to call my husband to pick me up from a nearby town. The relationship started gradually, both of us cautious, trying not to expect too much. I let Rachel dictate the pace of our reunion.

'Rachel came to stay for a weekend and met Philip and

Carolyn. Daniel had left home by this time and was living with his future wife. Strangely, he was the most upset by Rachel's appearance, seeing her as a threat to his place in the family. We met Rachel's boyfriend and visited her house. Her adopted parents had been unhappy when she needed to find her birth mother, worried she might be hurt by a further rejection, but when the reunion proved unthreatening, we all met at Rachel's house – two mothers talking about her as if she was not there, sitting between us on the sofa.

'It is now seven years since the reunion and I feel happy with my completed family. All my children are different, have contrasting needs and personalities, but I love them all. My husband and I have moved abroad and only Carolyn lives nearby. Daniel has given us our first granddaughter and two step-grandsons. Rachel visits regularly and this year came over with her adopted parents and partner for a long weekend.

'Daniel has matured into a responsible adult who we feel justly proud of, and Phil continues his laid-back approach to life as a teacher. Carolyn has coped with two years of chronic illness and is getting back on her feet again. Rachel is always the daughter we lost and have thankfully found again.

'Every adoption is different, every reunion hazardous. My advice to others is to take it slowly – don't expect too much too quickly. Try and imagine what the other person is going through. It can work if you really want it to.'

Birth fathers and grandparents

There are family members other than the birth mother on whom there is an impact if a child is lost to adoption. Birth fathers do not always know even that they have been responsible for a pregnancy and there is very little evidence to demonstrate whether they feel the same anguish and distress as birth mothers. Grandparents, however, may feel very strongly about the child.

Audrey

'My daughter got pregnant when she was just 16. Although we would have stood by her she decided to give the baby up for adoption because her relationship with the father had broken up. She went away to have the baby and refused to discuss any of her feelings with any of the family. When the baby was born, a boy, I went to see him but she wouldn't even hold him.

'I took him a teddy bear and some clothes and held him close every time I went to see him, but after five days he went to his foster family and I never saw him again. He was my first grandchild and I have never forgotten him. I think about him a lot; he will be 18 now. I have lit a candle for him on his birthday and each Christmas and I pray he is well.

'My daughter has another family now and she never talks about her first son. Maybe one day I will see him again.'

Experiences of adopted children

Although your thoughts are focussed on caring for your adopted child, a lot can be learnt from the experiences of adopted children:

Suzanna

'There are so many emotions involved in the process of growing up in an "adopted" family. For me it was a negative experience, in spite of being adopted by a loving, caring couple. The primal wound is like a scar that you are left with for life. That scar never goes away; you have to live with it. It goes everywhere with you. To me it was always a raw, painful experience, which I've carried on into adult life. Growing up in Ireland in the 60s didn't help.

'I feel that I am to blame for what happened to me. I am always trying to feel like a worthy person but am so full of insecurities and fears that I never succeed.

'I've been taking antidepressants since I was 17. They suppress a lot of emotions such as anger and pain. My biggest fear is of being abandoned and having no control over this. I am always seeking reassurance, which has got to be tough on my family.'

Many adopted children may never seek any more information about their birth parents. This may reflect the fact that some do not know they are adopted and some may feel no compunction to search at all.

Hugh

'I've known I was adopted for as long as I can remember, but it's never really bothered me. My adoptive mum and dad are my only mum and dad and I've no real curiosity about my other mum. I think my wife is more interested than I am.

'My adoptive parents were always very open with me and my adopted sister. They loved us and gave us a good home. I've got children of my own now but that hasn't changed the way I feel about trying to trace my biological mother.'

Others may start to search but find they have left it too late.

Kath

'I was adopted as a baby and in November 1997 I started searching for my roots. I discovered the following year that my birth mother had died six months earlier. I found that she had two sisters whom I have now met. I discovered that I had a half brother who was adopted by my birth mother's youngest sister. I'm excited that I am finally going to meet him as I always wanted a brother. I have spoken to him on the phone and now I shall meet him.

'I am so sorry that I never got to meet my birth mother but at least I have been able to fill in many of the gaps through meeting my aunts. I have learnt a lot about my mother and about my own history that has really helped me a lot.'

No matter how old the adopted child is when he comes into your life, the chances are that the life and love you provide for him will help him cope with the losses he has suffered before. If he has problems related or unrelated to the circumstances of his adoption you can only do your best for him.

The support network

There are many independent and state-supported bodies intended to provide support and information about adoption to those whose lives have been affected by adoption.

Adoption UK
Lower Boddington
Daventry
Northamptonshire
NN11 6YB
Telephone 01327 260295

Formerly known as Parent to Parent Information on Adoption Services, Adoption UK is a national self-help organization which is a registered charitable trust, run by adoptive parents and those with extensive experience of adoption, who offer support before, during, and after adoption to other adoptive and prospective adoptive parents.

With over 2500 family members with extensive experience of adoption of babies, older children, children with special needs, and sibling groups, there is a wealth of information and training support available. Member families include those who have adopted from overseas and those which include representatives from many ethnic and cultural backgrounds as well as gay and lesbian adopters.

Without doubt Adoption UK membership is vital for those who are embarking on the adoption process. They publish a quarterly journal comprising two parts, the first being an informative collection of letters and articles written by adoptive parents, features on issues relating to attachment, separation, and the effects of loss, abuse, and neglect followed by book and video reviews and notices of relevant training courses. The second section, 'Children Who Wait', lists children for whom adoption agencies are seeking families for either adoption or long term foster care.

Support services include links with other adoptive parents and children through a local adoptive parent volunteer co-ordinator as well as an opportunity to be part of the After Adoption Network.

Adoption UK is lobbying hard for improvements in adoption services, particularly addressing the issue of the number of times children are moved from one carer to another and pushing for a reduction in the period children remain looked after before they are placed for adoption or long term foster care.

Adoption UK have set up an experience resource bank called ERBIE, a computerized facility enabling them to link individuals and families together over a wide range of issues and situations. The office is staffed on weekdays between 11.00 am and 4.00 pm, and outside these hours there is an answering machine.

Publications include:

- *Resource Pack for Families Adopting a Child with a Disability;*
- *Checklist for Prospective Adopters;*
- *Guidelines for Teachers;*
- *Maintaining Links with Birth Families;*
- *Guidelines for a Letterbox for Adopted Children;*
- *Guidelines for Attending Meetings with Social Work Professionals;*
- *Adoption, Attachment and Development.*

There are also resource packs for racially mixed families and for families adopting a child who has been sexually abused, and they produce Adoption Day cards.

After Adoption in Wales
North Wales:
T'rbinwydden
Clayton Road
Mold
Flintshire
CH7 1ST
Telephone/Fax 01352 758829

South Wales:
Unit 1
Cowbridge Court
58–63 Cowbridge Road
Cardiff
CF5 5BS
Telephone 029 2057 5711

After Adoption Manchester
12–14 Chapel Street
Manchester
M3 7NN
Telephone 0161 839 4930/4932

After Adoption Yorkshire
31 Moor Road
Headingley
Leeds
LS6 4BG
Telephone 0113 230 2100

Another post-adoption support service which offers a search room, helping those who wish to search.

Barnardo's
Tanners Lane
Barkingside
Ilford
IG6 1QG
Telephone 020 8550 8822
Fax 020 8551 6870
Website www.barnardos.org.uk

Scotland:
Adoption Advice Service,
16 Sandyford Place,
Glasgow
G3 7NB
Telephone 0141 339 0772

British Agencies for Adoption and Fostering
Skyline House
200 Union Street
London SE1 0LX
Telephone 020 7593 2000

Scottish Centre:
40 Shandwick Place
Edinburgh
EH2 4RT
Telephone 0131 225 9285

British Agencies for Adoption and Fostering is a registered charity which helps children in need, finding new families for children who might otherwise grow up in the care of local authorities. They produce a wealth of training material and publications designed to help all those within the adoption circle. They can provide support at any stage in the life of a child who has been either fostered or adopted, from the earliest placement to the search for their birth family. There is a telephone information service.

Be My Parent is their bimonthly newspaper featuring news, features, photographs and profiles of children of all ages and backgrounds who need new permanent families through adoption or long term fostering. This is available to anyone who is interested, whether or not they have previous experience of adoption or fostering.

Twice a month BAAF publishes *Focus on Fives,* featuring information about children of five years or under, which is available only to approved adopters or foster carers.

They can put you in touch with social workers and placement officers from the voluntary bodies.

Catholic Children's Society (Nottingham)
7 Colwick Road
West Bridgford
Nottingham
NG2 5FR
Telephone 0115 955 8811
Fax 0115 955 8822
e-mail enquiries@ccsnotts.co.uk

The Catholic Children's Society has set up a project to help children aged three and upwards, of any or no faith, separated from their siblings through adoption. They can share their feelings and experiences through a website (www.nisw2.org.uk/project1618).

Jewish Association for Fostering and Adoption
Telephone 020 8952 3638 or 020 8207 6585

National Foster Care Association
87 Blackfriars Road
London
SE1 8HA
Telephone 020 7620 6400
Fax 020 7620 6401

National Organisation for Counselling Adoptees and Parents
112 Church Road
Wheatley
Oxfordshire
OX33 1LU
Telephone 01865 875000
Fax 01865 875686

A non-professional support group established to help adults handle their feelings about the effect of adoption on their lives. It provides opportunities for adopted people, adoptive parents and those people who have had a child adopted to talk freely with others who have personal experience of adoption. Some have also had special training and experience which can help individuals to resolve problems they may encounter.

Many adopted children use the resources of Norcap to help them trace birth family members. They publish a useful booklet *Searching for Family Connections* as well as providing an intermediary service.

Norcap is a self-funded group with a regular newsletter. Please write in the first instance enclosing a stamped addressed envelope for further information.

Natural Parents Network
3 Ashdown Drive
Mosley Common
Manchester
M28 1BR
Telephone 01273 307597

This group was set up to provide support and information to birth parents whose children have been placed for adoption. Many, who were left with little choice other than to place their children for adoption, feel intense grief at the loss of their children and furthermore at the absence of any information about them over the ensuing years.

Many of these birth parents try to seek their children at a later date, often after the first 18 years have passed. If, however, their children do not know they are adopted or do not seek to establish contact, there is little birth parents can do.

Many do not even know if their children are still alive. Through their newsletters, telephone help line and group meetings they support one another and lobby for changes in the law which will allow them greater access to information about their children and better education about their needs.

Our Place
139 Fishponds Road
Eastville
Bristol
BS5 6PR
Telephone 0117 951 2433
Fax 07070 610243

Our Place is a centre for families who foster and adopt children. It is a community-based charitable organization which offers support, education, and fun to parents/carers and their children.

At Our Place you can mix with others to share experiences in a friendly and informal atmosphere; join in activities such as art, music, drama, cookery; attend seminars and workshops addressing issues such as early child development, vulnerable and at-risk children, the education and emotional-behavioural needs of fostered and adopted children and their families; infant mental health; and other concerns of families with children in care.

Our Place is also for professionals who work with families caring for looked after and adopted children. Training for educational and other health/mental health professionals is available.

Many families who have adopted transracially and/or who have adopted from overseas have come to the centre to discuss the complicated issue of having children from varying ethnic and cultural backgrounds in their homes, and to meet with other families with similar experiences.

There are no charges at Our Place and anyone from any region is welcome to come. Our Place staff have a variety of qualifications and experience, but all have professional degrees.

Post Adoption Centre
5 Torriano Mews
Torriano Avenue
London
NW5 2RZ
Telephone 020 7284 0555

Advice Line 020 7485 2931 (staffed 10.00 am–1.00 pm Monday, Tuesday, Wednesday, and Friday; and Thursday evening 5.30 pm–7.30 pm)

Set up to meet the needs of both adults and children who experience problems arising from adoption, the Post Adoption Centre offers support, face-to-face counselling, family work and advice to individuals and groups.

Offering a post-adoption service to people, mainly in London and the South East, the Centre receives calls from over 3000 people each year, of whom approximately 24 per cent are adoptive parents, 23 per cent birth parents and 30 per cent adopted people.

There is a child and family service to help adoptive families in need, a mediation and contact service as well as access to a network of post-adoption trained counsellors.

West Midlands Post Adoption Service
92 Newcombe Road
Birmingham
B21 8BX
Telephone 0121 523 3343

National Social Services offices

England:
Social Care group, Children's services – Adoption
Department of Health
Room 233
Wellington House
133–155 Waterloo Road
London
SE1 8UG
Telephone 020 7971 4347/4084

Wales:
Public Health and Family Division (3)
2nd Floor
Cathays Park
Cardiff
CF1 3NQ
Telephone 029 2082 3145

Scotland:
Social Work Services Group
43 Jeffrey Street
Edinburgh
EH1 1DG
Telephone 0131 244 5480

Northern Ireland:
Department of Health and Social Services
Child Care Branch
Dundonald House
Upper Newtownards Road
Belfast
BT4 3SF
Telephone 028 9052 4769

Overseas adoption

The following addresses will be useful when it comes to applying
for the necessary approvals to adopt from overseas:

Foreign and Commonwealth Office
Legalisation Section
Ground Floor
Clive House
70 Petty France
London
SW1H 9HD
Telephone 020 7270 4063

Home Office Immigration and Nationality Department
Lunar House
40 Wellesley Road
Croydon
CR9 2BY
Telephone 020 8686 0688

International Social Services (United Kingdom)
3rd Floor
Cranmer House
39 Brixton Road
London
SW9 6DD
Telephone 020 7735 8941

Association for Families who Adopt from Abroad
1 Howard Road
Dorking
RH4 3HR
Telephone 01905 620005

Overseas Adoption Helpline
First Floor
34 Upper Street
London
N1 0PN
Telephone 020 7226 7666

Overseas Adoption Support & Information Services (Oasis)
Dan Y Graig Cottage
Balaclava Road
Glais
Swansea
SA7 9HJ
Telephone 01792 844329

A support group for people who want to adopt from abroad, with over 1000 members. There is a small charge for a general information pack and fact sheets on particular countries. All the money goes to children in need in third world countries. Support is offered by home-based volunteers.

The committee members, who have all adopted from overseas themselves, offer preparation seminars and conferences on overseas adoption. They provide information and support from the initial stages of considering overseas adoption through to the years after.

Parents Network for Post Institutionalised Children (PNPIC)
31 Court Lane
Wolstanton
Newcastle
Staffs
ST5 8DE
Telephone 01782 858915 (evenings only)

Adopted Romanian Children's Society
Telephone 01489 557353

Children Adopted from China
10 Woodcote
St Catherine's Drive
Guildford
GU2 5HQ
Telephone 01483 440370

This group provides support to families considering adopting a child from China and for those who have already done so.

Family Thais
Highfield House
Highfield Road
Horbury
Wakefield
WF4 4NA

For those considering adopting from Thailand.

The Adoption Contact Register

In 1991 the government introduced the contact register to enable adopted people and their relatives to register a wish to be put in contact with one another. They must both pay a small annual fee and there are two sections to the register, one for the adopted person and the other for any members of the birth family. Any information about a relative who wants to make contact is passed only to the adopted person so that she can retain control of the circumstances of any subsequent contact.
Telephone 0151 471 4586

Infertility

CHILD
Charter House
43 St Leonards House
Bexhill on Sea
East Sussex
TN40 1JA
Telephone 01424 732936
e-mail office@email2.child.org.uk

A national infertility support group providing support and information about all aspects of infertility and subfertility.

Recommended reading

There is a surprisingly large number of books covering many aspects of adoption from all points of view, including text books for those working in the field. If you were to buy all of them it would be an expensive exercise but there are many which will provide an enduring source of information as your adopted family develops. Social Services may have a limited library of books but financial restraints generally mean that they are not available for loan. Adoption UK also make a library of books available to members. All the following books are useful, but if your budget is limited those marked with an asterisk are strongly recommended.

*Archer, Caroline, & Adoption UK. *The First Steps in Parenting the Child who Hurts (Tiddlers and Toddlers)* and *The Next Steps in Parenting the Child who Hurts (Tykes and Teens)*. Jessica Kingsley, 1999. (Two books written by an experienced adoptive parent addressing separation, attachment and developmental issues for adopters. These books cover the complex range of difficulties with which children may struggle as a result of their early experiences. Drawing on both first hand experience and recent medical research, the author presents strategies to help parents deal with troubling behaviour, including sleep problems, anger, aggression and violence, addictive behaviours and self-harm among others.)

Brazelton, Barry. *Touchpoints: Your Child's Emotional and Behavioural Development*. Perseus Press 1994 and *Bruised before Birth*. BAAF 1995.

Chennells, Prue, & Morrison, Marjorie. *Talking about Adoption*. BAAF 1995.

*Fahlberg, Vera. *A Child's Journey Through Placement*. BAAF 1994.

Hicks, Stephen, & McDermott, Janet. *Lesbian and Gay Fostering and Adoption*. Jessica Kingsley Publishers 1998.

*Howe, David. *Adopters on Adoption*. BAAF 1996.

Keck, Gregory C. & Kupecky, Regina M. *Adopting the Hurt Child: Hope for Families with Special Needs Kids.* Pinon Press 1995. (This book is a must for those who know they have adopted a child who is hurting as a result of failed attachment. If you think your child may be suffering, even if adopted at a very young age, this book will help you recognize the signs and show you strategies that will help you.)

Morris, Ann, & Adoption UK. *The Adoption Experience: Families who Give Children a Second Chance.* Jessica Kingsley 1999.

Smith, Gerrilyn. *The Protectors' Handbook.* The Women's Press 1995. (An invaluable resource for parents who have adopted a child who has suffered sexual abuse.)

Thomas, Caroline, & Beckford, Verna. *Adopted Children Speaking.* BAAF 1995. (For those thinking of adopting an older child. Based on a limited study of children who have been adopted when they are older, explaining their own feelings and experiences.)

Verrier, Nancy. *The Primal Wound.* Gateway Press 1993.

Publications available in the United States include a regular bimonthly magazine, *Adoptive Families,* covering all stages of development, with recent research and useful articles. It is available from Adoptive Families of America, 2309 Como Avenue, St. Paul, Minnesota 55108.

The Internet and adoption

There is a considerable and valuable fund of information about adoption on the world wide web and while much of it originates in the United States it is none the less very useful. With most major search engines using 'adoption' as the key search word you will find information about support groups, people who are trying to trace other relatives, information about intercountry adoption and often interesting lecture material from many of the authors who have written books on adoption.

Index

abuse 40, 42; failed
    attachment 81–3; sexual 90;
    the traumatized child 85–8
Adopted Romanian Children's
    Society 66, 125
*Adopting a Child: A Guide
    for People Interested in
    Adoption* (Chennells and
    Hammond) 17
*Adopting the Child Who
    Hurts* (Keck) 83
adoption: first steps 10–13;
    legal process 36–8; recent
    social changes 2–3; as
    treatment for infertility 8–9
Adoption Act (1976) 14
adoption agencies 3–4;
    applying to 16–17, 20;
    assessment procedure 20–8;
    contesting 29; overseas 30;
    the panel 28–30
Adoption Agencies
    Regulations 14
adoption allowance 48–50
Adoption UK 17, 41, 43, 44,
    60, 115–16
Adoptive Families of America
    (magazine) 53, 128
adoptive parents: assessment
    procedure 20–8; attachment
    69–77; disabilities 40, 49;
    employment 19; immediate
    reactions to child's arrival
    67–8; institutional
    guidelines for 17–18; with

partner or single 2, 17–18;
    self-assessment 4–6; your
    own children 91
After Adoption 116–17
Archer, Caroline: *First Steps
    in Parenting the Child Who
    Hurts* 78
Association for Families who
    Adopt from Abroad 124
attachment 34–5, 78–90;
    disorders 71–7;
    institutionalized children
    61; normal processes
    69–71; noting signs of
    problems 80; older abused
    children 81–3
attention deficit and
    hyperactivity disorder
    (ADHD) 84–5

Barnardo's 117
Be My Parent 41, 50, 118
behavioural problems 42;
    emotional development
    81–3; school 51, 84–5; the
    traumatized child 85–8
birth parents: change of mind
    33; child's right to know
    32; consent only after six
    weeks 36–7; contact
    register 125; counselling
    15, 37; explanations and
    portrayals for children
    98–101; grandparents
    112–13; information about

131